Creative Writing For Adults:

Crafting Compelling Stories With Practical Methods For Building Plots And Memorable Characters

PUBLISHED BY Maya Linden

Table of contents

Introduction — Owning Your Lived Experience on the Page 4

Chapter 1 — The Premise Engine: From Spark to Logline 10

Chapter 2 — Theme Without Preaching: The Hidden Architecture 21

Chapter 3 — Character Systems: Desire, Wound, Mask 32

Chapter 4 — Relationship Geometry: Cast & Ensemble 44

Chapter 5 — Plot as Decisions: Choice Architecture 56

Chapter 6 — Structures to Steal (and Bend) 68

Chapter 7 — Time & Pacing: Narrative Clocks 81

Chapter 8 — Point of View & Voice: Access and Attitude 93

Chapter 9 — Scene Mechanics: Micro Tension That Never Lets Go 105

Chapter 10 — Revision Pipeline: From Rough to Relentless 116

Introduction — Owning Your Lived Experience on the Page

You already own a lifetime of story lab work—meetings, arguments, victories, losses—quietly training you to write. Every awkward conversation that replayed in your head on the drive home, every negotiation that hinged on one sentence, every small win that changed the way you saw yourself—all of it is narrative material. You've already done your apprenticeship. The job now is not to invent something from nothing, but to recognize that the stories you've lived contain the same architecture as the ones you want to tell. This book is about converting that reservoir of experience into craft—systematically, playfully, and sustainably.

Most adult writers arrive here with one of two worries: that it's too late, or that their life isn't "interesting" enough. Both are illusions. Experience doesn't need to be cinematic to matter; it only needs to be understood. In fact, the adult writer's secret weapon is perspective. You've already seen patterns—people repeating mistakes, systems breaking under pressure, relationships flourishing or failing for predictable reasons. That pattern-recognition is the raw material of theme. When you translate it to the page, you move beyond imitation and into insight. The younger writer may have energy and novelty; the older one has data, emotional calibration, and endurance. The trick is learning how to turn those invisible assets into visible story mechanics.

This book isn't about waiting for inspiration or following formulaic templates. It's about process fluency—the kind that lets you move from a spark to a structured draft without killing momentum. The creative process, like any other professional practice, benefits from workflow design. You already know this from work or parenting or running your household: habits reduce friction. Systems protect creativity from chaos. Here, you'll learn to apply that same logic to storytelling through a few essential tools that you'll use from first idea to final revision.

Before diving into the deeper chapters, it helps to see how to use this book. Think of it as both a workshop and a field manual. Each chapter ends with a **Quick Method**—a practical checklist or small experiment designed to translate theory into motion. Try them immediately. Don't wait to feel "ready." Momentum builds mastery faster than overthinking.

Keep three core documents open, digital or analog—it doesn't matter which.

The first is your **Plot Grid**, a living blueprint that lets you track your story's architecture without drowning in outline theory. You'll build it across four rows—your A plot, your B plot, your Antagonist's through-line, and your Theme Beat—and stretch it across the key structural moments: Inciting Incident, First Threshold, Midpoint, Second Threshold, Climax, and Aftermath. This grid is not a prison; it's scaffolding. It keeps your story upright while you improvise inside it.

The second is your **Character Engine Card**, a compact diagnostic for the human core of your story. Every major character gets one. On it, you'll define their Desire, Wound, and Mask—the triad that generates both motivation and tension. Then you'll chart their Signature Actions (the things they do automatically), their Pressure Tests (moments that expose their fault lines), and their Price of Change (what they must lose to evolve). When you fill this out, you stop writing puppets and start writing people.

The third document is your **Scene Thermostat**, your moment-to-moment calibration tool. Each scene should contain a Goal, an Opposition, a Ticking Element, and a Value Shift—something that changes from start to finish. You'll also define an Exit Problem: what unresolved tension propels the reader into the next scene. If a scene lacks any of these, you'll know it's decorative, not functional. And decorative scenes are where drafts bloat and stories stall.

If that sounds mechanical, that's the point. The paradox of creativity is that constraint breeds freedom. The more reliable your tools, the more daring you can be with content. Once you know how to stabilize your structure, you can chase the risky emotional truths that make fiction worth reading.

The Adult Advantage: Transferable Skills → Story Power

Writing is rarely a blank-page act; it's an act of translation. And as an adult, you've spent years translating—between bosses and clients, partners and children, plans and realities. Every time you decoded someone's tone in a meeting, or framed feedback to prevent defensiveness, or negotiated a compromise, you were running small simulations of character dynamics. You already know how people protect their vulnerabilities, how they disguise motives, how they reveal truth by accident. That is character craft.

The key is to **mine your professional and personal history** as data, not diary. Start with what you've observed repeatedly. Maybe you've seen loyalty traded for speed, or competence punished by bureaucracy, or love eroded by distraction. These are thematic patterns—evidence of human cause and effect. Keep a "pattern ledger" where you jot these down. Later, you can flip one into a premise: what if loyalty itself became dangerous? What if speed turned into a moral test? This is how mature storytelling begins—not from spectacle, but from insight sharpened into dramatic tension.

Then there's **conflict navigation**, something adults do constantly. In fiction, conflict is story. A scene without stakes or opposition is just information. But when you apply what you've learned from real-world conflict—identifying stakeholders, understanding incentives, predicting escalation—you can design scenes that feel psychologically true. You already know that people rarely argue about what they're actually arguing about; they argue about identity, validation, fear. Translating that to dialogue instantly adds subtext.

And finally, there's **system thinking**, the ability to manage complex processes over time. Many adults already operate in project cycles—planning, executing, reviewing. The same cycle applies to creative writing: idea → outline sketch → discovery draft → diagnostic pass. Treat it like any other long-term project. This framing dissolves perfectionism. A draft isn't a referendum on your talent; it's a phase in an iterative system.

Sustainable Practice Without Sacrifice

Creativity isn't a luxury reserved for those with open schedules. It's a discipline that thrives on rhythm. The most sustainable writing practices are designed around how your actual life works, not how you wish it did. That's why this book leans on the concept of **focus loops**—compact, repeatable sessions that train your brain to associate certain cues with deep work.

Choose a ritual: the same chair, the same beverage, the same playlist. These become your **trigger**. Then write for a defined block—30 to 60 minutes, aiming for progress, not perfection. That's your **action**. When the timer ends, step away. Reward yourself with a short walk, a stretch, or something sensory. That's your **reward**. Over time, the loop becomes automatic. The brain loves predictable reward structures; they make consistency effortless.

Meanwhile, build an **idea inbox**—a digital folder or notebook divided by tags: Premise, Character, Scene, Line. Whenever a thought surfaces, drop it in immediately. Once a week, review and sort. You'll find that this small act of capture converts random inspiration into an organized archive. You'll never again lose a spark because you were "too busy."

Most writers quit not from lack of skill but from friction. They can't find the right file, or their backup failed, or they don't know where to start. So eliminate friction. Create a default template that opens ready for a new scene. Set up auto-backups. Use a simple sprint timer. When starting costs nothing, resistance disappears. Sustainable practice is built on removing excuses, not adding effort.

The Toolset You'll Use Throughout

The **Plot Grid, Character Engine Card**, and **Scene Thermostat** are not gimmicks—they're thinking aids. They translate intuition into visible structure so that you can revise intelligently instead of by gut alone.

The **Plot Grid** will keep you honest about pacing and parallel arcs. It ensures your antagonist's logic evolves alongside your protagonist's growth and that your theme isn't just a moral but an evolving question embedded in each beat. Seeing all this at once reveals imbalance early, before you waste chapters.

The **Character Engine Card** exposes what most drafts hide: that behavior is driven by contradiction. A wound creates a mask, a mask creates signature actions, and those actions generate both empathy and conflict. The "price of change" is what makes arcs satisfying. Without it, your story resolves intellectually but not emotionally.

The **Scene Thermostat** keeps micro-tension alive. Every scene, however quiet, must shift the temperature of the story. Maybe a relationship warms, maybe trust cools, maybe the reader's certainty flips. That value shift—measured from one state to another—is what creates forward momentum. When you see it charted, you'll start to sense pacing by instinct.

You'll come back to these tools constantly. They are the grammar of your process—the way you translate big ideas into line-level choices. Once mastered, they fade into the background. You won't have to think about them consciously any more than you think about grammar while speaking. But they'll be there, ensuring your storytelling stays coherent even when your imagination runs wild.

In the end, **creative writing for adults** is not about reclaiming youth or chasing originality; it's about recognizing the story-shaped intelligence you already use daily and turning it toward art. The difference between life and literature is not content but framing. You've lived the research. Now it's time to write the report—not as a diary, but as design. This book will walk you step by step through that translation, giving you the tools to move from experience to expression, from idea to finished story. Draft fast. Revise deliberately. Ship often. The rest is iteration.

Chapter 1 — The Premise Engine: From Spark to Logline

If you can say your story in one breath, you can build it in one draft. That's the power of a sharp premise: it isn't a tagline, a mood, or an idea in search of justification. It's the DNA that determines everything—the world, the tone, the cast, even the rhythm of sentences. Weak premises produce beautiful fragments that can't cohere. Strong premises generate momentum; they attract characters, conflict, and theme like magnets. The paradox is that most writers start too vague, believing they'll "discover" the premise along the way. In reality, discovery is much faster when the spark is already under pressure. You need a creative engine that forces opposites together until they combust. That's what the "What If" factory does.

1.1 The "What If" Factory

A story begins with friction—two incompatible elements that can't coexist but must. "What if" is how you trap that contradiction inside a single sentence. It's not wishful thinking or random combination; it's design. You're building a miniature physics experiment, one that proves something must change. "What if a lawyer discovered the only way to save her client was to destroy the evidence herself?" Already, you have collision: law and ethics, self-interest and justice. A premise that contains paradox naturally generates plot because it demands resolution. Without friction, you're left with atmosphere, not story.

The fastest way to find paradox is **cross-pollination of constraints**. Take two ideas that don't belong together and force them to share oxygen. Start with a genre—say, a legal thriller—and fuse it with a profession or environment that introduces moral or procedural conflict: "hospice nurse." Then add a destabilizer: "forged consent forms." The sentence "A hospice nurse uncovers forged consent forms that could implicate her in a patient's murder" immediately carries moral complexity and urgency. You can feel the pressure already; this world will yield difficult choices. Each addition—genre, profession, pressure—narrows possibility until what's left is tension.

Constraint is not limitation; it's leverage. A premise becomes compelling not by adding more elements, but by discovering the right incompatibility. If you keep stacking ideas, you dilute. If you choose two that genuinely strain against each other, you ignite. "Fantasy + accountant" works because imagination and precision rarely coexist. "Romance + meteorologist" becomes interesting only when weather mirrors emotional volatility. The "What If" factory doesn't generate randomness; it manufactures paradoxes that promise consequence. Every strong premise is a contract with the reader that this tension will evolve, that something vital is at stake.

Another technique is **flipping a norm or trope**. Familiar structures comfort the reader, but inversion wakes them up. Reverse competence or power. What if the villain is brilliant and the hero unprepared? What if the savior doesn't believe in salvation? What if the story expected to unfold in a courtroom takes place in a hospice or a submarine? Location, authority, morality—all can be inverted. When you flip expectation, you create oxygen for originality. The same way music gains energy through dissonance, story gains energy through reversal. You're not discarding convention; you're repurposing it.

Consider how setting redefines tension. A spy thriller set in wartime Berlin already has stakes, but we've seen that. Move it to a small-town nursing home, and the familiar tropes mutate. Surveillance becomes caretaking; secrets hide behind routine. The reader can't predict outcomes because context has changed. Inversion breathes life into overused patterns without abandoning the scaffolding that makes them work. You can flip character dynamics, too: make the mentee more ruthless than the mentor, the detective emotionally blind, the child wiser than the adults. Each reversal shifts gravity.

Once you've fused paradox and flipped expectation, the final lever in the "What If" factory is **the ladder of extraordinariness**—a method for escalating premise without breaking plausibility. Start with something ordinary, relatable, and specific. Then climb the ladder by adding a resource limit— a countdown, a depletion, or an eroding trust. Time, oxygen, food, love, loyalty—whatever your story's currency is, drain it. Limitation breeds propulsion.

Imagine a simple scenario: "A man tries to apologize to his estranged daughter." Now add a constraint: "He has one phone call from prison." The situation tightens. Add another: "The call is being monitored, and the person listening has their own history with him." Now the premise hums. Each rung up the ladder adds urgency while keeping the emotional truth intact. The extraordinary grows naturally from the ordinary because limitation clarifies value. The less of something we have, the more it matters.

The ladder also protects against inflation—stories that escalate through spectacle rather than tension. If your premise relies on larger explosions instead of deeper stakes, it exhausts rather than engages. Resource limits refocus attention on the human. In a disaster film, the countdown isn't to the meteor's impact; it's to the moment when someone must choose between saving the world or the one person they love. The external limit (time, space, oxygen) presses the internal limit (faith, courage, morality) until something yields. That's where emotion hides: not in scale, but in compression.

When you feel your "What If" wobbling under abstraction— when it starts sounding like a concept rather than a situation— run it through the three filters: paradox, inversion, limitation. Ask: what two values collide here? Which expectation have I reversed? What resource is running out? If your premise answers all three, it can carry a novel.

A useful exercise is to test potential premises aloud. A good one fits in a single breath without confusion. If you must pause to explain or qualify, it's not yet focused enough. "A scientist who clones her dead son" already implies emotional chaos, ethical questions, and urgency. You don't need to say more. "A journalist discovers a conspiracy" tells us nothing unique; we need the paradox that defines it—what kind of journalist, what personal limitation, what impossible conflict. "A deaf journalist uncovers a conspiracy hidden in sound" suddenly crackles. Constraint (deafness) and paradox (investigating what she cannot hear) create fascination.

Another test: remove one element and see if the engine still runs. If it does, you may not have compressed tension tightly enough. A strong premise collapses when you subtract any component because each part is structural. In "A hospice nurse uncovers forged consent forms," remove "hospice" and you lose intimacy and moral pressure; remove "forged consent forms" and you lose crime; remove "nurse" and you lose vulnerability. The story's power lies in the combination.

The "What If" factory works best when you treat idea generation as a disciplined game rather than divine visitation. Write down ten combinations quickly. Don't judge them yet.

Cross-pollinate professions, settings, and stakes until sparks fly. The ones that feel strange or even absurd often hold the most promise, because strangeness is just unfamiliar logic waiting to prove itself. A "ballet thriller about industrial espionage" sounds ridiculous until you realize both worlds hinge on choreography, secrecy, and discipline. Suddenly it's a mirror, not a joke.

While generating, stay alert for the emotional heartbeat beneath the concept. Premise without heart is gimmick. Ask why this contradiction matters to you personally. The "What If" isn't just external—it's the thematic skeleton of what you believe about people. The hospice nurse premise might be about guilt versus mercy; the deaf journalist about isolation versus discovery. The paradox you build for plot often mirrors a paradox you carry internally. When that alignment happens, the story has heat.

In revision, your premise becomes the diagnostic tool for everything else. When a subplot drifts, check whether it serves the central "What If." When character motivation falters, ask how it ties to the paradox you began with. The premise is not a marketing hook—it's the gravitational center of meaning. If it's strong, the rest of the craft decisions simplify because they orbit naturally.

To summarize the spirit (though not the mechanics) of this chapter: the "What If" factory doesn't ask you to be a genius; it asks you to be a scientist of tension. Mix ingredients until the reaction can't be contained. Find collisions that reveal truth, flip familiarity until it surprises, and constrain freedom until urgency appears. Do this, and you'll never again face the terror of the blank page. You'll have an engine humming beneath you, ready to convert spark into story—a single breath of contradiction that can sustain an entire book.

1.2 Logline Formula & Anti-Formula

If a premise is the spark, the logline is the distillation—the controlled flame you can hold in your hand without getting burned. It's the sentence that tells you, in miniature, what your story is about, why it matters, and why anyone should care. The most powerful stories, from *Casablanca* to *Breaking Bad*, can be expressed in a single breath not because they're simple, but because they've been compressed to their essence. Writing that single line isn't about marketing; it's about clarity. When you can articulate your story's DNA, you've already built its skeleton.

A logline, at its most functional, is an engineering diagram of tension. It is not a tagline or a summary—it's a problem in motion. The core template captures that movement: *When [flawed protagonist] must [urgent goal] to [protect X], they [take risky action] but [escalating complication].* Every clause in that structure exists for a reason. The "when" introduces the triggering event—the moment the status quo cracks. The "must" defines urgency, a pressure that forces the protagonist into motion. The "to protect X" reveals motive: not just what they want, but why they can't walk away. The "risky action" shows agency, and the final "but" signals the arrival of opposition, the generator of conflict.

If any one of these pieces is weak, the whole narrative collapses. For instance, if your protagonist isn't flawed, they won't grow. If the goal isn't urgent, the story drifts. If the stakes aren't specific, the reader won't invest. And if there's no escalating complication, the plot becomes static. Each piece of this grammar forces you to make a choice that prevents vagueness. "A woman tries to find herself" isn't a story; it's a mood. But "When a burned-out hospice nurse discovers her late patient's forged consent forms, she must expose the fraud before the company buries the evidence—and her career" has direction, pressure, and consequence.

The formula's power lies in the way it focuses your attention on necessity rather than ornament. However, the danger of formulas is that they can become cages if used mechanically. Every story has its own rhythm, and sometimes clarity requires breaking the rule while keeping its spirit. That's where the **anti-formula** comes in: the deliberate reshuffling of components to foreground what truly defines your narrative. Some stories are world-first. Think of *The Handmaid's Tale*—the premise doesn't start with a character's action but with a society's rule: "In a dystopian theocracy where women are enslaved for childbirth, one handmaid risks everything to reclaim her name." Here, the world itself is the inciting event; the "when" is implicit in the setting.

Other stories are antagonist-first. *Moby-Dick* begins not with Ishmael's personal flaw but with Ahab's obsession. Sometimes your premise needs to announce the pressure before introducing the one who will bear it: "When an unkillable creature stalks a stranded crew across an icy wasteland, their leader must choose between saving them or finishing the hunt." Inverting the order shifts emotional weight. You're still following the core grammar—goal, risk, complication—but the emphasis now lies on the external threat that defines the internal journey.

Breaking the formula doesn't mean ignoring clarity. It means choosing the most revealing entry point. Ask yourself: what's the emotional engine? If your story hinges on moral tension, open with the protagonist. If it hinges on circumstance or discovery, open with the world. If it hinges on dread, open with the antagonist. What matters is that, by the end of one sentence, we understand both *why* the story must happen and *what might be lost* if it doesn't.

To test your logline, try the **identity swap**: replace your protagonist's name or role with "anyone." If the sentence still works, it isn't sharp enough. "When a man must stop a killer to save his family" could describe a thousand thrillers. But "When a deaf sound engineer discovers her son's kidnapper uses low-frequency tones to trigger panic attacks, she must weaponize her silence to fight back" can't describe anything else. Specificity breeds distinction. The reader's curiosity blooms in proportion to how tightly your premise could only exist for this one person, in this one context.

A logline should also hum with contradiction. Human interest arises from tension between opposites—desire and fear, competence and vulnerability, power and guilt. When your logline contains an internal friction, the story writes itself. Consider: "When an idealistic public defender must prove her client's innocence, she discovers he's guilty—and decides to save him anyway." That paradox doesn't just sell the plot; it encodes the theme. You can feel the moral combustion waiting to ignite.

Ultimately, the goal of a logline is not to advertise but to diagnose. It's the moment you stop wandering and start building. If you can summarize your story in one breath, you can outline it in one sitting and draft it in one season. That's what professional writers mean when they say, "Get your premise right, and the rest is just logistics."

1.3 Stress Testing the Premise

Once your logline stands, you must test it like a bridge design before anyone drives across it. Many writers fall in love with an idea's novelty but neglect to check whether it bears narrative weight. A premise is only as strong as the tension it can sustain under pressure. That's where stress testing comes in: pushing your idea from every angle until it either fractures or reveals its structural integrity.

The first test is the **Antagonist Test**. Ask: does the opposition arise inevitably from the premise, or did you bolt it on afterward? A strong story grows conflict organically from its own seed. If your logline is "A doctor must expose a hospital cover-up before more patients die," the antagonist shouldn't be a random corrupt executive tacked on for convenience. The opposition should be baked into the very system she's trying to save—perhaps her mentor, perhaps the institution's moral inertia. The most resonant antagonists aren't villains; they are embodiments of the protagonist's blind spots. They believe they're right. If you can't describe your antagonist's logic in a way that would make sense to them, your premise isn't yet self-sustaining.

Next comes the **Setting Pressure Test**. Too often, stories could take place anywhere. That's a sign the environment isn't pulling its weight. A strong setting multiplies risk and limits options. If your protagonist could simply walk away, the reader will too. Imagine the same premise in different locations: a corporate whistleblower in a glass tower versus one stationed on an offshore rig. The latter is instantly more claustrophobic. Or take a domestic drama and set it on a long-haul spaceship instead of a suburban cul-de-sac; suddenly, every emotional choice has physical consequences. The right setting is an accelerant—it traps your characters where change is unavoidable.

Then there's the **Promise of Change**, the often-overlooked but vital component. Every story, regardless of genre, sells a transformation. Readers invest time not for spectacle but for movement—from ignorance to understanding, isolation to connection, cowardice to courage. The promise of change is the contract you make with them in the first act. If nothing will be different by the end, there's no reason to start. The trick is to define the before/after axis as early as possible. What state of value—love, freedom, truth, power—is at stake, and how will it shift? The reader doesn't need to know *how* the change will occur, only that the narrative guarantees it.

When you've mapped these three pressures—antagonist, setting, and transformation—you can perform the final simulation: imagine removing any one of them. Does the premise still hold? If you can swap the antagonist, relocate the setting, or erase the transformation without breaking the story, your idea is still too generic. Real tension is interdependent. The best premises form closed ecosystems—every element feeding the others. In *Jaws*, for instance, the antagonist (the shark) is inseparable from the setting (a seaside town) and the transformation (a sheriff conquering fear). Alter one variable, and the entire premise collapses.

A stress test also helps you predict burnout. Some ideas can sustain a short story but not a novel. Others have enough torque for a series. To measure longevity, ask: how many new questions does this premise generate after its initial setup? If you can list at least five escalating "what happens when…" scenarios, you've got long-form potential. If you can only think of one, the premise may be better suited for a short form. This doesn't devalue it—it simply tells you where it belongs.

Another valuable test is emotional endurance. Can the premise continue to surprise you after ten drafts? If it still provokes moral unease or wonder when you retell it, you've found a core that will keep readers hooked too. But if you feel nothing but fatigue, the story may be built on gimmick rather than truth. The most enduring premises are not just clever—they're charged with something the writer themselves hasn't fully solved. That unsolved tension becomes the current that drives the work.

Finally, remember that testing is not cynicism; it's devotion. You stress the premise not to break it, but to learn its breaking point. Once you know that, you can build the rest of the novel around protecting and exploiting that tension. A weak premise demands constant patchwork later—contrived twists, artificial stakes, inflated melodrama. A strong one, once verified, carries you effortlessly through the grind of drafting.

When your premise has passed these trials, you'll feel a click of inevitability, a quiet conviction that the story could not unfold any other way. That's when you know you're ready to move from the premise engine to the plot machine—from spark to structure. And that's the moment the page stops being blank and starts being alive.

Chapter 2 — Theme Without Preaching: The Hidden Architecture

Theme is the question your plot refuses to stop asking. It's not a statement you tack onto the end of your story, nor a moral you deliver from a pulpit—it's the gravitational pull shaping every choice your characters make and every pattern your reader subconsciously detects. The best themes are invisible engines; they hum beneath the surface, turning repetition into resonance. When done well, a reader doesn't say, *"I learned a lesson."* They say, *"I felt something echo."*

Theme, more than any other craft element, separates story from anecdote. Plot tells us *what happens*, but theme tells us *why it matters*. It's the deeper geometry beneath your narrative, the invisible math that organizes emotion, imagery, and meaning into coherence. To write theme effectively is not to declare, but to discover—to let the story interrogate its own premise until the reader emerges changed. In this way, theme is the story's ongoing question, not its answer.

2.1 Mapping a Thematic Web

The process of developing theme begins not with philosophy but with inventory. Start by asking: what keeps reappearing? Before you write a manifesto or thesis, notice your obsessions. Every writer has them—recurring ideas, symbols, and contradictions that slip into every project. Maybe it's the cost of loyalty, the fear of aging, the tension between privacy and truth. Don't suppress these; chart them. They're the fingerprints of your inner story engine.

Imagine your theme as a web—each thread a motif that carries emotional charge. Motifs are the concrete expressions of abstract meaning: objects, gestures, colors, weather, sounds, repeated phrases. A cracked watch might represent time lost or a broken promise. Rain might shift from cleansing to oppressive depending on the character's growth. A recurring gesture—say, a father checking his cufflinks before lying—can evolve into a quiet language of guilt. By inventorying these elements, you begin to visualize how the story communicates subtextually, without a single lecture line.

Every motif has to earn its keep by evolving. Repetition alone is decorative; repetition that transforms is thematic. Think of it like musical variation—the same note played at different emotional volumes across acts. Suppose your motif is light. In Act One, light could symbolize surveillance—harsh fluorescents in a hospital or interrogation room. In Act Two, it could represent clarity or truth—the flashlight beam cutting through fog. In Act Three, it might become exposure—the same light that once revealed now endangers. The motif matures with the character's understanding. The reader feels this shift, often without noticing, and the cumulative effect is depth.

To manage this web, you can literally build an **image system**. Some screenwriters, particularly in visual mediums, create spreadsheets where every major motif is assigned a column. Each row represents a scene, and every time the motif appears— whether as object, color, or sensory cue—they mark it. This may sound mechanical, but it's liberating. You'll start to see where your imagery clusters too densely or disappears for long stretches. The pattern becomes visible, like veins under skin. By tracking your motifs, you ensure that your story's thematic bloodstream keeps circulating.

Writers of prose can adapt this method. Create a margin tag or comment every time a recurring symbol appears. As you revise, skim those tags. Are you building progression or merely echoing yourself? For example, if a door appears multiple times, does its meaning change—from barrier to invitation, from safety to trap? Each shift in symbolic function parallels your protagonist's inner journey. What changes in the motif mirrors what changes in the human. That is the essence of theme in motion.

Another way to build the web is through **thematic pairing**—placing opposing images or ideas in dialogue across your story. If your central question is about control versus surrender, pair recurring symbols that mirror both sides: a clenched fist and an open hand, a locked room and a free horizon. As these symbols recur and transform, they create visual tension that mirrors your narrative tension. The theme doesn't need to be stated; the reader feels the pull between extremes.

But beware of forcing motifs. They must arise naturally from the world you've built, not from an imposed idea. A theme can't be superimposed like wallpaper—it has to grow from the soil of your premise. If your story began with a "what if" rooted in moral tension, its imagery should emerge organically from that tension. In a story about honesty, you might find mirrors, reflections, or glass. In a story about survival, perhaps metal, blood, or hunger. Let the world speak its own symbols, and you'll find the thematic structure already waiting beneath the surface.

Once you've identified your motifs, tag every scene where they appear. This is where the **motif presence map** becomes invaluable. For each scene, note which motif surfaces—visually, audibly, or emotionally—and how its meaning has shifted since the last time it appeared. This technique ensures recurrence without redundancy. If you find a motif repeating without evolution, revise to either deepen its context or replace it. A repeated image with no progression is noise; one that transforms is narrative glue.

Let's take an example. Imagine a story centered on the theme of moral compromise. Early on, a character notices the sound of a ticking clock while falsifying a report—a minor lie. Later, when committing a larger deception, the same ticking grows louder, almost unbearable. By the climax, the clock stops—either literally or symbolically—marking the point of no return. The motif has traveled from background noise to moral reckoning. This evolution gives your theme shape without a single speech about ethics.

Another powerful dimension of the thematic web is **emotional color**. Each motif can carry a tonal charge—hopeful, ominous, bittersweet—that modulates the reader's experience. The color red, for instance, might begin as a symbol of vitality and end as one of guilt. The repetition teaches the reader subconsciously to associate emotion with imagery. Film directors exploit this constantly—think of the recurring blue in *Moonlight* or the use of green in *The Matrix*. Prose writers can do the same through texture, metaphor, and sensory recall.

Theme mapping also clarifies when to use restraint. Not every page should scream meaning. Thematic power often comes from spacing—allowing silence between echoes so that each recurrence feels earned. A motif's absence can be just as telling as its presence. If your story revolves around communication, the scene without any dialogue might carry the most weight. If your motif is sound, then sudden quietness can jolt the reader awake. Think of theme as rhythm: repetition and rest creating pattern.

When designing your thematic web, remember that consistency isn't monotony—it's coherence. Readers crave pattern recognition; it's hardwired into cognition. We find satisfaction not in surprise alone but in the click of realization when repetition resolves into meaning. Your job is to choreograph those realizations so the reader discovers the theme rather than being told it. That's why tracking motifs visually can transform your revision process. You'll start to sense how even a color choice or minor prop contributes to your story's philosophical spine.

Theme without preaching means trusting imagery more than exposition. It means allowing the story's emotional logic to do the heavy lifting. When a reader feels the theme before they can name it, you've succeeded. You're not writing sermons; you're building resonances. Every object, every gesture, every repeated word is a tuning fork. Together, they form a field of vibration beneath the narrative. When the reader turns the final page, that vibration lingers. They might not know why, but they'll feel that something true has been said—not aloud, but through pattern.

Mapping a thematic web is not an academic exercise; it's a way of thinking about storytelling as architecture. You're laying down invisible girders that hold the emotional structure in place. The motifs are the crossbeams, the image systems the wiring, the recurring colors the light that spills through each room differently depending on time of day. If you've done it right, the reader will never see the blueprint—they'll just feel the balance, the integrity of design. And when they leave the building of your story, they'll carry its echo, still resonating in their chest, without ever realizing how you built it.

2.2 Value Conflict Ledger

If theme is the gravitational pull beneath your story, values are the tectonic plates that grind against each other to generate that heat. Every meaningful narrative arises from competing goods, not from the battle of good versus evil. That's where the **value conflict ledger** comes in—a conceptual tool for mapping the opposing forces that drive your theme without collapsing into moral slogans. A story that preaches resolves too easily; a story that endures forces readers to wrestle with irreconcilable values.

Mercy versus justice. Freedom versus safety. Truth versus loyalty. Every scene becomes a stress test for where those opposites meet, clash, and mutate.

To build this ledger, start by naming the value pair at the heart of your story. Choose poles that exist in dynamic tension rather than binary opposition. "Love versus hate" is too blunt to generate nuance; "love versus self-preservation" is better. The key is that both sides must be defensible. If one pole feels entirely right and the other entirely wrong, the audience won't feel torn—they'll simply root. The best themes place us in ethical suspense, making us feel the cost of choosing either side. The power of *Les Misérables*, for instance, comes from watching Inspector Javert embody justice so completely that mercy feels like chaos, while Valjean embodies mercy so deeply that justice feels cruel. Both men are right—and both are wrong. That's the ledger in motion.

Once you've defined your poles, imagine them as opposite ends of a continuum. Your protagonist might begin near one extreme, while supporting characters occupy other coordinates. A mentor might inhabit the middle ground; an antagonist might sit at the opposing pole. These placements aren't labels—they're tensions waiting to ignite. When these worldviews collide in action, you get friction without caricature. The antagonist isn't evil for its own sake; they're simply loyal to a different virtue. A journalist who values truth above loyalty isn't villainous when she exposes her friend's secret; she's consistent with her position on the ledger. This consistency breeds complexity, allowing every conflict to feel inevitable rather than contrived.

Scenes become experiments inside this moral grid. Each interaction tests not whether a character wins or loses, but which value gains temporary dominance. A courtroom drama might test justice and mercy by forcing a lawyer to decide whether to reveal exonerating evidence that will destroy her career. A love story might test freedom and commitment by giving each partner a reason to betray the other for self-realization. The ledger ensures that conflict is never arbitrary—it's always a reflection of the theme. Every argument, every betrayal, every reconciliation moves one square on the grid.

The most potent moments arise when the story forces **compound choices**—decisions where either option costs something sacred. These choices dramatize theme far better than dialogue ever could. "Save X or reveal Y" becomes a crucible: protect a loved one and betray your principles, or expose the truth and destroy the person you love. Compound choices remind us that life rarely offers moral purity, only trade-offs. When you construct these dilemmas with care, the theme stops being abstract and becomes embodied in human pain.

In your ledger, you can visualize this tension by creating four quadrants. Imagine mercy on one axis and justice on the other. A character high in mercy but low in justice might enable wrongdoing out of compassion. One high in justice but low in mercy might enforce punishment without empathy. The middle ground—where both operate in balance—is rarely stable; events constantly push characters out of equilibrium. Your protagonist's arc often traces a diagonal movement across this chart—from imbalance through crisis toward integration. They don't abandon one value for the other; they learn how to hold both without breaking.

This ledger also prevents **cartoon villainy**. When you understand the antagonist's value alignment, you can write them as sincerely as the hero. They aren't blocking the protagonist because they're cruel—they're protecting a different sacred thing. In a story about privacy versus transparency, the journalist who exposes classified data isn't evil, nor is the agent trying to silence her righteous. They simply occupy opposite poles of the same moral field. The reader feels empathy for both, which intensifies engagement.

To maintain balance, revisit your ledger as you draft. Each major scene should nudge the conflict along the continuum. Ask: which value dominated this scene? Did it shift? Did the characters pay a cost for choosing one over the other? If the answer is always the same, the story stagnates. You need reversals—moments when mercy leads to harm, when justice saves, when the moral arithmetic refuses to simplify. That oscillation keeps the theme alive.

In revision, trace each character's trajectory across the ledger. A satisfying narrative rarely ends with victory; it ends with clarity. The protagonist learns not which value is superior, but what balance they can live with. The ledger helps you see whether that transformation feels earned. Did the story truly pressure both poles, or did it quietly endorse one all along? If you find that your protagonist was right from page one, your theme hasn't evolved—it's preached. The ledger demands humility: the willingness to let your own assumptions face trial inside your fiction.

Ultimately, the value conflict ledger turns theme from something *said* into something *tested*. Instead of declaring "mercy is better than justice," you invite the reader to witness how mercy can destroy and justice can redeem. You let them feel the tension without dictating the resolution. That's what separates art from argument.

2.3 Beat Theme Integration

Once your thematic web and value ledger are in place, the next challenge is integration—ensuring that theme isn't an afterthought sprinkled over plot, but the current running through every beat. Each major story beat—inciting incident, midpoint, climax—should either deepen, challenge, or reverse the theme.

Theme integration is the art of designing change at every structural hinge so that the narrative's architecture mirrors the moral inquiry beneath it.

Start with the **inciting incident**. This is where your theme first appears as question rather than statement. Something in the protagonist's world destabilizes their moral equilibrium. If your theme is about freedom versus belonging, the inciting event might force the protagonist to choose between loyalty to a group and independence. The event need not state the theme—it simply activates it. Readers sense the question in the conflict's shape, not in exposition.

By the **first threshold**, the protagonist commits to a path that unconsciously favors one value over the other. The story then proceeds to test that allegiance. At the **midpoint**, introduce a revelation that redefines the theme—perhaps what the protagonist thought was virtue now looks like delusion. This is the thematic inversion point: the moment when the narrative's "moral weather" changes. If the first half of the story seemed to argue for justice, the midpoint begins to show mercy's necessity. The shift feels earned because it emerges from consequence, not correction.

Each beat becomes a dialectic: action, consequence, and new understanding. Instead of treating theme as something external to plot, treat it as feedback—the character makes a choice aligned with one pole of the ledger, experiences fallout, and must recalibrate. In this way, plot becomes philosophy in motion.

Avoiding sermonizing requires **argument beats**—moments where two intelligent sides debate without either being entirely right. The tension lies in the fact that both positions hold truth. A courtroom speech that condemns corruption is dull if unopposed; a cross-examination that reveals the cost of integrity electrifies the scene. The best thematic arguments are not monologues but collisions of logic and emotion. When readers feel themselves swayed by both perspectives, they experience the theme as living tension, not a message.

To make argument beats work, embed them in action. A disagreement during a crisis lands harder than one in a café. External stakes compress internal conflicts, forcing characters to articulate values under pressure. This naturalizes theme—readers don't feel lectured; they feel implicated. In *The Godfather*, every thematic beat about family versus morality occurs in the context of a power move. The conversation is never abstract; it's always blood on the table.

Theme also ripples through **foreshadowing and callback**. Thematic foreshadowing is not about predicting plot twists; it's about establishing moral weather that will later shift. Introduce a small image early—a bird trapped in a cage, a child watching a storm—and reintroduce it later, transformed by cost. When that image reappears changed, the reader feels the story's moral evolution without explanation. A caged bird escaping in the final act means more than any line about freedom. These callbacks tie emotional threads, turning isolated moments into a unified experience.

One subtle but powerful technique is to let the **world itself** respond to the thematic journey. The setting can evolve with the protagonist's moral state: light growing softer as understanding deepens, architecture decaying as integrity collapses, weather mirroring turbulence or calm. These aren't coincidences; they're reflections of the story's pulse. When done carefully, such shifts operate below awareness, giving the reader the sense that everything—characters, world, and imagery—is in moral conversation.

At the climax, the theme reaches synthesis. But synthesis doesn't mean resolution. The protagonist faces a choice that embodies the question raised at the beginning. They act not to declare truth but to live with ambiguity. This is the "value payoff" moment, when both poles of your ledger converge under impossible pressure. Whether they choose mercy, justice, or something in between, the reader feels the cost because every prior beat prepared it.

Finally, in the aftermath, revisit your motifs one last time. Let one of them return altered—perhaps a broken object now repaired, or a color once oppressive now peaceful. These **quiet callbacks** act as emotional punctuation, confirming that change occurred not just in circumstance but in meaning. The reader closes the book sensing that something invisible has rebalanced, even if they can't articulate how.

Integrating theme across beats is like tuning an instrument— you're aligning vibration, not reciting theory. Every story moment hums at a frequency; your job is to make those frequencies harmonize around the central question. When you succeed, theme ceases to be an intellectual layer and becomes felt structure—the hidden architecture that makes a story linger long after its last page.

Chapter 3 — Character Systems: Desire, Wound, Mask

Memorable characters are algorithms of desire under pressure. Every line they speak, every mistake they make, every silence they hold traces back to a pattern of wanting, fearing, and pretending. Plot may give a story its motion, but character gives it gravity—the invisible mathematics that turns sequence into consequence. When readers say a character "feels real," what they're responding to is not complexity for its own sake but coherence under stress: the sense that each decision grows inevitably from a private logic. To write such people, you must understand the machinery that drives them—the dynamic triad of **Desire, Wound, and Mask**.

3.1 The Desire–Wound–Mask Triad

A character's *Desire* is what they consciously pursue; their *Wound* is the historical injury that distorts that pursuit; their *Mask* is the strategy they've built to survive the wound. These three forces operate like a closed system of cause and effect, generating the energy that propels the story. Without them, you have behavior without reason. With them, even the smallest gesture feels charged with implication. The key is learning to calibrate the interplay among the three—how the wound warps desire, how the mask conceals it, and how, under pressure, the mask begins to crack.

Start with Desire, because that's what readers can see. It's the visible goal, the metric by which progress is measured. A detective wants to solve the case, a mother wants to protect her child, a student wants to prove herself. But desire alone doesn't make character—it makes ambition. What transforms ambition into story is the Wound beneath it, the emotional debt driving the urgency. Perhaps the detective once failed a victim and is now haunted by guilt. Perhaps the mother lost a child before and now overprotects. Perhaps the student was told she'd never amount to anything and now mistakes validation for worth. The Wound is the engine's scar tissue: it explains the overreaction, the obsession, the blind spot.

The Wound rarely announces itself. It's encoded in behavior— the little rituals of self-protection that become the Mask. The detective's sarcasm, the mother's control, the student's perfectionism: all are shields against the original injury. The Mask "works" for a while; it delivers success, praise, even love. But the cost of safety is authenticity. The longer the character hides behind the Mask, the more alienated they become from their true needs. The story begins when the Mask, under the heat of the plot, stops functioning.

This is where most writers fall short—not in inventing backstories but in dramatizing *pressure*. The reader doesn't care about the Wound until they see its defenses tested. That's why you must script **mask-slip moments**—brief, specific scenes where the character's façade fails to hold. A mask slip is not a confession; it's a micro-tear in control. It can be a snapped reply, a trembling hand, a laugh too long, an unguarded look. The audience may not know why it happens, but they feel its truth. These moments are the fault lines where the inner story leaks into the outer one.

Think of a surgeon who prides herself on composure. In Act One, she cracks a joke during crisis—a coping mechanism. In Act Two, the same joke falls flat, her voice catching. By Act Three, silence replaces humor entirely; the Mask no longer fits. This progression tells the story of a soul under duress without a single speech about trauma. The slip reveals evolution. It's not the

Wound that changes—it's the strategy for concealing it that disintegrates.

To make the Mask tactile, anchor it in something the audience can see or touch—a uniform, a ritual, a prop, a phrase. These emblems externalize identity, allowing you to stage transformation visually. A police badge, a wedding ring, a pair of perfectly shined shoes—each can represent the persona the character performs. When the story reaches its turning point, the act of removing or losing that emblem becomes a rite of passage. In *Casablanca*, Rick's tuxedo and cigarette are his armor of cynicism; when he sends Ilsa away, that armor no longer defines him. The object's absence becomes narrative shorthand for rebirth.

It's tempting to define the Mask as deception, but it's more accurately adaptation. The character's persona once *saved* them. That's why they cling to it. A soldier's discipline might have prevented collapse in war; in civilian life, it prevents intimacy. A comedian's humor might have defused childhood violence; as an adult, it deflects love. The Mask's tragedy is its double edge: it was once medicine, now it's poison. Your job is to write the story that forces recognition of that shift.

When plotting, map how Desire, Wound, and Mask intersect across the story's structure. In the beginning, Desire drives action while the Mask keeps the Wound hidden. Midway through, circumstances pressure the Mask until it cracks, revealing glimpses of the Wound. By the end, the protagonist must either shed the Mask or collapse beneath it. This choice—the courage to face pain or the compulsion to repeat it—is the true climax of character. The external resolution mirrors the internal one. If the detective solves the case but still can't forgive himself, the story ends in irony, not healing.

This triad also helps you avoid the trap of sentimentality. When you know the Wound, you don't need melodrama; quiet gestures suffice. A character polishing her late husband's glasses every night can convey grief more powerfully than a page of exposition. Similarly, when you know the Mask, you can stage conflict through contrast: what happens when the character meets someone who refuses to play along? If the perfectionist is suddenly admired for failure, the Mask loses oxygen. That dissonance sparks revelation.

In ensemble stories, the Desire–Wound–Mask model creates chemistry. Each character's triad should interact frictionally with others'. One person's Mask triggers another's Wound; one person's Desire threatens another's stability. These crosscurrents generate organic tension. You no longer have to manufacture conflict—it emerges naturally from incompatible psychologies. In *The Breakfast Club*, each student's defense mechanism (Mask) irritates the others until collective vulnerability forces truth. The group's shared Wound—alienation—transcends their surface differences.

You can test whether your characters are alive by swapping their Masks. Would your plot still work if the stoic became the joker, the romantic became the cynic? If yes, the psychology isn't yet specific enough. A living character would distort the story's geometry. Their choices, fears, and rituals must feel so idiosyncratic that no one else could occupy their slot without rewriting the narrative's DNA.

Desire, Wound, and Mask also define *voice*. Dialogue isn't only about what's said—it's about what's avoided. A Masked character speaks in coded language, evading vulnerability. Their diction, rhythm, and humor all serve self-protection. As the story progresses, speech patterns loosen; syntax mirrors emotional exposure. That's how readers sense growth without narration: the way the character talks evolves before the character admits why.

Every writer has their own version of these forces in life. Desire is your ambition. Wound is the disappointment you swore you'd never feel again. Mask is the persona you built to survive your profession, your family, your failures. Writing characters through this triad requires empathy born of self-awareness. You don't have to confess your own story, but you have to recognize the pattern. The closer you look at yourself, the more truthful your characters become.

Ultimately, the Desire–Wound–Mask system is not a formula but a way of seeing. It allows you to write people as systems in motion rather than static archetypes. Every act, whether noble or foolish, becomes understandable once you trace it to its origin. Readers forgive a character's mistakes when they glimpse the pain beneath them. That's what makes fiction moral without being moralistic: it teaches compassion through understanding, not instruction.

When the Mask finally falls—whether through surrender, exposure, or loss—the story's emotional circuit completes. The Desire that once ran on fear is purified by insight. The Wound that once defined the character now integrates into wisdom. The plot resolves, but the reader feels something larger: the recognition that identity itself is a fragile equation between wanting, hurting, and pretending. You've given them not a hero, but a mirror. And in that mirror, they see themselves—cracked, luminous, and still becoming.

3.2 Contradiction Stacks

A great character isn't defined by consistency but by contradiction. What makes someone feel real on the page is not how logically they behave, but how they contain incompatible truths that coexist uneasily within them. The contradiction is the pulse that keeps them human—it's the friction between what they say and what they do, between what they want and what they fear. Flat characters move in straight lines; living ones move in spirals. And the tighter those spirals wind under pressure, the more powerfully readers feel the heartbeat of the story.

The idea of **contradiction stacks** means layering these tensions intentionally—not as decorative quirks, but as fault lines designed to collide. Each major character should carry at least three contradictions that will eventually interfere with one another. The goal isn't to make them unpredictable; it's to make them inevitable in their complexity. Real people aren't mysteries—they're equations with too many variables. The writer's job is to balance them long enough for the story to expose where the math breaks.

Let's say you're writing a ruthless negotiator who also volunteers at a children's hospital and is obsessively neat. On paper, these traits seem unrelated, maybe even arbitrary. But under the surface, they reveal a system of emotional compensation. The negotiator's ruthlessness masks guilt; volunteering is an unconscious atonement. Their need for order is how they manage chaos. As long as life remains under control, these contradictions coexist peacefully. The story begins when control fails—when a messy, morally ambiguous situation forces the compartments to bleed into each other.

That's the essence of writing contradictions: **collision, not cataloging**. A contradiction only matters if the story creates conditions for it to self-destruct. Maybe the negotiator's client turns out to be the same hospital that relies on her volunteer work. Now her empathy threatens her ambition. Maybe the obsessive neatness breaks down when she's forced to work with someone disorganized who exposes her fragility. The more you let the contradictions grind against each other, the more pressure builds.

The plot doesn't need to manufacture tension; the character provides it from within.

The most enduring literary figures are built from contradiction stacks so tight they hum. Think of Jay Gatsby: a dreamer obsessed with purity who makes his fortune through corruption. Or Michael Corleone: a war hero who becomes the very monster he sought to protect his family from. Their contradictions don't just define personality—they define destiny. Each story's tragedy or triumph depends on which contradiction wins.

To keep contradictions from becoming caricatures, anchor them in cause and context. Ask yourself: *what emotional logic makes these opposites coexist?* A man who preaches humility but collects luxury watches isn't necessarily hypocritical; maybe he grew up poor and needs constant proof that he's escaped scarcity. A woman who saves animals but can't sustain human friendships isn't cold; perhaps she finds the unconditional love of animals safer than the risk of betrayal. Contradictions don't cancel each other—they justify each other. When readers sense that hidden logic, empathy replaces judgment.

One of the most subtle ways to dramatize contradiction is through **signature tells**—physical or linguistic patterns that surface when the character's control slips. These tells act like stress sensors; they reveal internal conflict without exposition. A calm politician who flits his eyes whenever he lies, a soldier who straightens his sleeves before disobeying orders, a teacher who overexplains when she feels ignored—these are micro-confessions of humanity. The reader learns to recognize them instinctively, often before the character does.

A good tell should feel organic to personality, not invented for symbolism. It's the sort of unconscious tic that belongs only to that person, born from the same internal contradiction that defines them. The trick is subtlety: don't underline it, don't announce it. Let it emerge naturally and repeat under escalating stress. The repetition builds psychological rhythm. When the reader sees that gesture late in the story—after the character has evolved—it will carry weight. A tell once born of anxiety might, by the end, signify release.

Contradictions also determine chemistry between characters. Opposites attract not because they're different, but because each person's contradiction resonates with the other's. The disciplined surgeon falls for the reckless artist because both secretly envy what they repress. The cynic befriends the idealist because together they approximate wholeness. The more you understand your characters' internal divides, the more authentically you can connect or antagonize them.

In revision, check your contradiction stacks for dramatic potential. Are they visible only in description, or do they generate conflict on the page? Do they evolve under pressure, or remain static? The best stories track contradiction collapse—the moment when two opposing drives can no longer coexist. That's when the character must choose which part of themselves to kill. Fiction, at its core, is about internal civil wars. Contradiction stacks give you the map for where those battles take place.

3.3 Arc Typing & Trajectories

Once you've built the inner machinery of Desire, Wound, Mask, and layered the contradictions that make it volatile, you must decide what kind of motion this engine will produce. Character arcs aren't decorations tacked onto plot—they are the shape of transformation itself, the emotional geometry through which a story moves from question to consequence. Understanding your character's **arc type** clarifies not only what changes, but what it costs.

There are three fundamental trajectories: the **positive change arc**, the **steadfast or flat arc**, and the **negative or disillusionment arc**. Each operates by the same rule: pressure reveals truth. What differs is how the character responds to that truth—whether they grow toward it, hold firm against it, or break under its weight.

In a **positive arc**, the protagonist begins in moral or emotional blindness and moves toward self-awareness. The story dismantles their Mask and replaces it with integration. Think of *A Christmas Carol*: Scrooge's greed isn't cured by ghosts—it's confronted by consequence. Each visitation forces him to relive the cost of his denial until empathy becomes the only escape from despair. The plot applies escalating pressure nodes—moments where staying the same becomes intolerable. By the end, change is not a choice but a survival instinct.

In a **steadfast or flat arc**, the protagonist doesn't change internally—the world does. This arc suits stories of moral conviction or ideological resistance. The character's belief is tested by increasingly punishing circumstances, and their integrity transforms those around them. Think of *To Kill a Mockingbird* or *Erin Brockovich*: the protagonist's steadfastness exposes corruption, revealing the gap between who we are and who we claim to be. The emotional engine still runs on pressure, but its output is endurance rather than metamorphosis.

The **negative arc**, or disillusionment arc, is the mirror image of the first. Here, the character begins with hope or innocence and descends into cynicism, addiction, or despair. But this isn't mere tragedy—it's revelation inverted. The truth destroys rather than redeems. In *Macbeth* or *Breaking Bad*, ambition exposes moral rot. The character gains knowledge but loses soul. The negative arc reminds readers that enlightenment isn't always liberating; sometimes it's fatal.

Choosing an arc type isn't about genre—it's about worldview. What kind of moral gravity does your story obey? If redemption feels true to the world you've built, aim for positive change. If endurance feels nobler than surrender, hold steady. If corruption feels inevitable, let decline be the answer. The important thing is internal logic: the arc must arise naturally from the same forces that define your theme.

Regardless of arc type, you must identify **pressure nodes**—the moments when the price of stasis spikes. Without these nodes, transformation feels unearned. Pressure nodes can be external (a betrayal, a death, a revelation) or internal (a realization, a loss of illusion). They function like tightening screws, increasing torque on the character's contradictions until something snaps. Early in the story, the cost of staying the same might be embarrassment; later, it's death or alienation. The rising cost curve is what turns a situation into a story.

The most profound arcs also track the **Price of Change**—what must be lost for transformation to occur. Growth is expensive. To become someone new, the protagonist must surrender something they once believed essential: a relationship, a delusion, a privilege, a protection. The Price of Change is the tollgate at the climax. The reader must feel its weight, because only sacrifice validates transformation.

In a redemption arc, the price might be self-image: the hero must admit weakness to gain humanity. In a steadfast arc, the price is comfort: the hero loses belonging to preserve truth. In a negative arc, the price is conscience: the hero achieves their goal but forfeits themselves. These costs define the emotional budget of your story. Every meaningful change has a receipt.

To visualize trajectory, imagine the character as an object in orbit. At the start, gravity (the Wound) pulls them inward. The Mask provides just enough velocity to keep them circling safely.

Each pressure node increases gravitational force until the orbit decays. The fall—whether into truth, ruin, or transcendence—is the arc. Your job isn't to nudge them; it's to calculate the forces that make falling inevitable.

When designing arcs, resist tidy catharsis. Real transformation is asymmetrical—growth in one area often demands regression in another. A protagonist who becomes brave might lose tenderness; one who learns honesty might lose community. The messiness of aftermath makes the change believable. Endings that feel too "clean" betray human reality; we rarely emerge from crisis purified—we emerge rearranged.

Finally, connect the arc back to the thematic web from earlier chapters. If your story explores mercy versus justice, then every stage of the character's trajectory should modulate that tension. Each pressure node should confront them with both poles until, at the climax, they must choose which value to embody. The arc isn't separate from theme—it's how theme breathes.

When you finish mapping an arc, read your story backward. Does every major scene reflect a different stage of internal alignment? Can you trace, step by step, how pressure shapes perspective? If the answer is yes, your character lives. They are not a puppet moved by plot, but a being whose psychology dictates motion. The story doesn't carry them—they carry the story.

At its best, a character arc feels less like design and more like fate. You, the writer, are simply the cartographer of inevitability—charting how desire, wound, and mask collide through contradiction, until the only possible ending is the one that feels both surprising and true. When readers reach that point, they don't think, *"The character changed."* They think, *"Of course."* And that quiet click of recognition—the sense that human behavior, however contradictory, finally makes emotional sense—is the most powerful sound in fiction.

Chapter 4 — Relationship Geometry: Cast & Ensemble

Plots accelerate when relationships change status. A story doesn't move because time passes or events occur; it moves because bonds between people evolve—tighten, fracture, reverse. Every scene that matters pivots on a shift in relationship geometry: a friend becomes a rival, a mentor becomes an obstacle, an enemy becomes an uneasy ally. Those changes are the hidden physics of storytelling, the emotional gravity that pulls characters into new orbits and forces recalibration. You can stack subplots, twist timelines, or expand settings, but if the relationships remain static, the narrative will always feel inert. The audience stays not for the events, but for the tension of watching loyalties rewire in real time.

4.1 Ally/Opponent Grid

To understand how relationships shape momentum, you must first see them as dynamic systems rather than fixed roles. The **ally/opponent grid** is a tool for charting that movement. Imagine a spectrum that runs from full alliance to full opposition—with intermediary stations like rival, skeptic, or nemesis. Every major pair of characters exists somewhere on that line, but crucially, their position can and should shift as new information enters the story. The grid is not a taxonomy; it's a living map. A character may begin as an ally at dawn and end as a nemesis by nightfall, and the reader feels every degree of that rotation as emotional velocity.

Each pair on this spectrum should share one contested resource—something both value but cannot possess without tension. It might be literal, like money, land, or credit; or intangible, like loyalty, truth, love, or safety. The contested resource gives each interaction weight. Without it, relationships drift into pleasant but empty chatter. Even the most affectionate partnership needs a live wire—a subtle competition, a suppressed grievance, a diverging goal—to create the electricity of narrative interest.

In great ensemble fiction, every relationship forms its own microclimate. Some are tropical—volatile, fast to storm and clear. Others are polar—cold, enduring, glacially shifting over time. What unites them is that each has a pressure differential. When one side changes temperature—say, by gaining new knowledge or suffering a betrayal—the weather between them changes. The more sudden the shift, the stronger the narrative wind.

Consider how this operates in *The Godfather*. At the start, Michael and his father Vito share warmth but distance: Michael is the outsider, loyal but disengaged. As the plot unfolds, every event—each assassination, each moral compromise—repositions them on the grid. The father becomes a mirror, the son a shadow. By the end, when Michael assumes the throne, they have swapped positions entirely. That reversal doesn't just change the relationship; it redefines the moral axis of the film. The emotional shock of recognition—seeing who Michael has become—lands because we've felt the incremental slide from ally to successor to rival.

When writing your own pairs, focus less on dialogue and more on alignment. Ask yourself: where do they stand on the grid at the start of the story, and where will they stand by the end? The difference between those two coordinates is your relationship arc. Once you know the direction of travel—toward alliance or opposition—you can structure turning points that dramatize each stage of that migration.

A **turning scene** is the hinge on which relationship status flips. It's not necessarily loud or violent; it's the moment when one piece of truth detonates quietly between two people. Maybe an ally discovers a lie. Maybe an enemy shows unexpected mercy. Whatever the case, it's the event that redefines terms of connection. The reader should feel the ground tilt—the instant when affection curdles or suspicion softens. These scenes are the emotional keystones of your ensemble; without them, relationships stagnate into labels.

Crafting a turning scene requires precision. The revelation must feel both inevitable and devastating—something that could only have been hidden by the intimacy of the relationship itself. A stranger's betrayal stings; a friend's betrayal shatters. The deeper the shared history, the higher the voltage when truth hits. That's why you must establish the old equilibrium first—show the texture of alliance before breaking it. Trust only hurts when we've seen it lived in.

Equally powerful are reversals toward connection. A long-time rival who becomes an ally offers one of storytelling's most satisfying arcs because it dramatizes mutual transformation. Two characters can only move closer when each surrenders an illusion about the other. The scientist learns the outlaw's code of honor; the outlaw learns the scientist's patience. Every compromise is a revelation: to cooperate, they must first see one another clearly. When opposites align, the story's moral fabric tightens.

One mistake many writers make is tracking relationship beats as identical to plot beats. The two are linked, but not synonymous. The plot might require a heist, an election, a voyage; the relationship beat is the emotional adjustment that the event causes between people. You can plot an action-heavy chapter, but if the relational status hasn't shifted by the end, the scene contributes little to the story's emotional arc. Tracking these beats separately allows you to layer complexity. An external victory might coincide with an internal fracture, or a shared loss might forge unexpected solidarity. The best scenes accomplish both simultaneously: moving the plot while deepening or reversing bonds.

Try envisioning your story as a matrix where each character's row intersects with every other's column. Each cell contains the current temperature of that pair—ally, rival, opponent, or nemesis—and the degree of change since the last interaction. During drafting, update the grid after each major beat. You'll start to see emergent patterns: triangles of tension, alliances forming and dissolving, loyalties migrating like weather fronts. This view transforms ensemble writing from chaos into orchestration.

For instance, in a political thriller, you might begin with a tight alliance between two aides working for the same candidate. But one leak, one compromise, and the lines blur. Perhaps the first aide values loyalty, while the second values truth. When the scandal breaks, both believe they're saving the campaign, but their definitions of "saving" diverge. By tracking their shifts— ally to rival to reluctant opponent—you create rhythm without adding extraneous subplots. The tension *is* the story.

What makes ensemble fiction especially potent is how these relationship arcs overlap. Each character's emotional journey refracts through others, forming interference patterns of trust, betrayal, and reconciliation. The reader experiences the ensemble as a living organism, its chemistry constantly adjusting to new stimuli. Think of *Game of Thrones* or *Succession*—not just sprawling plots but ecosystems of allegiance, every conversation altering the balance of power. The thrill comes from watching geometry rearrange itself in real time.

The most satisfying ensembles also exploit asymmetry. One character may perceive alliance while the other perceives rivalry.

This misalignment generates friction because affection becomes one-sided, loyalty misread, hostility misjudged. When the truth finally aligns—when both characters recognize they've been on different coordinates all along—the revelation lands like an earthquake.

To sustain this complexity, each relationship needs its own **contested resource**. Without something tangible or emotional at stake, no amount of witty dialogue will keep the connection alive. It might be control of a secret, approval from a shared mentor, or the affection of the same third person. The resource ensures that every interaction has subtext. Even when characters cooperate, there's a silent tug-of-war underneath. The resource isn't always external—it can be psychological, like the need to be right, the hunger to be admired, or the fear of abandonment. As long as both want something that can't be shared equally, tension endures.

When building your cast, think of it as architecture. Each relationship is a structural beam; the story's integrity depends on how they connect. Too many beams running parallel create redundancy; intersecting ones create strength. In revision, cut relationships that duplicate function—two characters offering identical reflection or resistance. Each connection should pressure the protagonist differently, illuminating a new facet of their contradictions. The best casts form a prism: the same soul refracted through many perspectives.

Finally, remember that relationships, like characters, must evolve under pressure. If two allies remain perfectly aligned from first chapter to last, they risk becoming furniture. The audience yearns for friction—the ache of almost-breaking, the risk of loss. Even love stories, perhaps especially love stories, depend on temporary misalignment. Tension is not the opposite of connection; it's proof of it. The strength of any bond is measured by how much strain it can bear before it either breaks or transforms.

When you've tracked your ally/opponent grid across a full narrative arc, you'll begin to notice that plot and emotion are not separate rails—they're the same track seen from different angles. Every twist in the story corresponds to a relational torque somewhere in the ensemble. The heist fails not because of logistics, but because trust decayed. The revolution succeeds not because of strategy, but because belief synchronized. The geometry of your cast—who trusts whom, who envies whom, who forgives whom—is the true map of story motion.

So as you write, think less in terms of scenes and more in terms of relationships recalibrating. Ask, after every chapter: who now owes whom? Who trusts less, who loves more, who feels replaced? Those invisible exchanges of emotional currency are what make the plot accelerate. The story breathes not when events happen, but when relationships change status—and the grid, alive with shifting coordinates, becomes your proof that it's still in motion.

4.2 Triangles & Third Elements

If relationships are the arteries of a story, triangles are its pulse. They compress emotion, concentrate tension, and force characters to define themselves through choice. A dyad—two people locked in connection—offers stability. Add a third element, and equilibrium collapses into orbit. The geometry becomes dynamic; each move reconfigures loyalties. Whether the triangle is romantic, political, or moral, it exists to sharpen stakes. A loves B, but B needs C. A protects C, but C betrays A. These patterns create narrative combustion because every gain for one is a loss for another.

Triangles reveal character faster than exposition ever could. When two people share a secret in the presence of a third, their alliance becomes visible without words. When one character's loyalty divides between two others, the reader senses fault lines before dialogue confirms them. This is the power of triangulation—it makes the unsaid vibrate. You can feel it in every great ensemble, from *Casablanca*'s quiet despair to *The Hunger Games*' layered allegiances. The triangle works because it mirrors the contradictions of real human life: we're rarely pulled by one loyalty alone.

The craft lies not in arranging triangles for gossip or melodrama, but in **pressure design**—building situations where each corner must act, and every action isolates them further. A political thriller might stage it as a senator torn between a loyal aide and a lobbyist who holds compromising information. A family drama might frame it as a child caught between divorcing parents. The emotional force arises from compression: each scene narrows the corridor until someone must betray, confess, or flee.

To make a triangle compelling, resist symmetry. A perfect triangle is static; one side must always carry more tension. Perhaps A needs B more than B needs A, or C doesn't realize they're the hinge. Imbalance is the source of motion. The most devastating scenes occur when that imbalance suddenly reverses—when power or knowledge shifts and the neglected vertex becomes the center of gravity. The writer's job is to choreograph these reversals so that each new configuration feels inevitable yet surprising.

But not all triangles are composed solely of people. The most nuanced narratives introduce **third elements**—forces or presences that operate like silent characters. The law, tradition, a deity, a social code, even the weather can function as a third participant, shaping what can and cannot be said. In *Atonement*, it's not another person but the weight of class and wartime duty that drives the wedge between lovers. In *Moby-Dick*, the sea itself is the third element, mediating every encounter between Ahab and his crew. These external forces add texture and density; they make private relationships accountable to public systems.

The presence of a third element transforms the simplest conversation into moral theatre. Imagine a scene between two lovers arguing in a church. The building itself listens. Its silence, its symbolism, its echo—all become part of the emotional tension. When you stage such moments, the goal is to make the environment complicit. The walls, the wind, the clock ticking in the background—each one can take a side without speaking. The third element's silence often speaks louder than any character's dialogue.

This technique of **silent triangulation** works especially well in stories about secrecy, repression, or taboo. A law that forbids certain speech, a tradition that demands conformity, a weather event that traps characters together—all these external conditions magnify intimacy by limiting escape. The more inescapable the third element, the tighter the emotional compression. When the pressure peaks, small gestures—an unspoken glance, a half-step forward—acquire the magnitude of plot twists.

To craft a powerful triangulation scene, focus not on dialogue but on orientation. Who faces whom? Who looks away? Which direction does the silence lean? In film, blocking carries this weight; in prose, you can translate it through spatial and sensory cues. If A speaks to B while C listens unseen, the air itself becomes charged with imbalance. The reader feels the geometry before understanding it. This nonverbal choreography transforms static exposition into dynamic tension.

Triangles also sustain long-form storytelling. In serial fiction, where relationships must evolve over hundreds of pages, triangulation prevents stagnation. As alliances shift, triangles reconfigure, creating a self-renewing engine of drama. Today's confidant becomes tomorrow's threat; the outsider becomes the moral center. Each new combination of three recalibrates meaning. The trick is to let these reconfigurations happen through revelation, not coincidence. When one character learns something the others don't, the shape changes naturally, and readers lean in, trying to predict who will align next.

Beyond character, triangles allow theme to become visceral. Every value conflict—truth versus loyalty, mercy versus justice—finds its most potent form when three entities embody those poles. One represents principle, another affection, the third survival. The protagonist's heart, intellect, and fear are externalized across three bodies. Each scene then becomes a test of integration: which value will they privilege, and what part of themselves will that cost?

Perhaps the most crucial insight is that triangles don't need to end in resolution. Sometimes the most haunting conclusion is perpetual imbalance—the sense that these three lives will continue to orbit one another, bound by shared gravity. Closure is less satisfying than resonance. A triangle left humming with tension stays alive in the reader's mind long after the book closes.

4.3 Network Effects

Once individual triangles are in motion, the story begins to develop a social geometry of its own. This is the realm of **network effects**—the phenomenon where every new relationship changes the value of all others. In ensemble fiction, characters don't evolve in isolation; they evolve through contact, friction, and miscommunication across a web of connections. Each tie has ripple effects that extend beyond the immediate pair or trio. The writer's challenge is to orchestrate these ripples without losing clarity.

The most efficient way to harness network effects is through **rotating point of view**. Each shift of perspective changes the reader's understanding of who holds power, truth, or illusion. When one character hides information and another misinterprets it, the reader occupies a privileged yet unstable position—knowing more than any single participant but never enough to predict outcomes. This oscillation creates narrative electricity. The ensemble becomes a hall of mirrors, reflecting motives back and forth until the true pattern emerges.

Think of *Rashomon* or *The Affair*, where the same events refract through multiple lenses, each altering the moral calculus. The genius of this technique lies not in contradiction for its own sake but in revelation through partiality. No one sees the full network. Each viewpoint reveals bias, shaping the reader's allegiance minute by minute. By the time truth surfaces, we've experienced empathy for all sides, even those who stand opposed.

To manage complexity, you need a sense of **invisible architecture**—a map of who knows what, when, and why it matters. This doesn't have to live in the text, but you should keep it in your process notes like a conspiracy board: strings connecting motives, secrets, debts. Information asymmetry is storytelling gold. When two characters interact while holding different versions of reality, subtext crackles. The reader senses double meanings everywhere—what's spoken versus what's withheld, what's assumed versus what's feared.

Network effects also reward **long-range planting**. Early in the story, seed small interactions between unlikely characters—what might seem like a throwaway conversation between the janitor and the CEO, the student and the rival's spouse. Later, when crisis hits, those faint connections bloom into **hidden bridges**—unexpected alliances that feel both surprising and earned. Readers love to realize that what looked like background was actually scaffolding. These payoffs depend on patience: the bridge must be invisible until the moment it's crossed.

The art of managing an ensemble is to give every player a vector. Not everyone needs equal page time, but everyone needs direction—something they're moving toward that intersects, collides, or interferes with others' goals. This directional energy creates a sense of inevitability. Even minor characters feel alive because they generate ripples; they're not furniture, they're weather systems influencing the central climate.

To maintain balance across this complexity, some writers keep an **ensemble ledger**—a behind-the-scenes document tracking scene count, participation, and influence. It's not about quotas; it's about rhythm. If one character dominates too long, the web collapses into a line. Alternating focal points restores multidimensionality. The ledger also helps you see who's overdue for consequence. A character who triggers change but never faces fallout creates narrative imbalance. When everyone's actions rebound somewhere in the network, the world feels self-regulating, alive.

In well-built ensembles, the story's climax is not a single explosion but a synchronized chain reaction. Every subplot ignites another, every alliance triggers a reckoning. The resolution doesn't come from one protagonist's victory but from the network's reconfiguration. A lie finally exposed forces two others to tell truths. A single act of sacrifice redeems or condemns everyone it touches. This orchestration gives the ending scale— it feels communal, not isolated.

Network effects also let you explore how systems, not individuals, generate meaning. A workplace novel, for instance, can use ensemble dynamics to expose how ambition, envy, and hierarchy circulate like current through a circuit board. Remove one resistor and the entire network overheats. The focus shifts from who did what to how power flows. The same logic applies to families, governments, even ecosystems. The pattern of relationships becomes the story's argument about interdependence.

From a stylistic standpoint, managing networks demands compression. Scenes must do double duty: advance multiple relationships at once, deliver information to some characters while concealing it from others, and alter the reader's understanding of alignment. The dialogue of ensemble fiction is layered like counterpoint in music—one voice carrying melody while another hums tension beneath.

The greatest reward of this structure is the cumulative emotion it produces. When a late revelation ricochets through the network, the reader feels a surge of recognition: *of course* this affects everyone. It's the emotional equivalent of watching a flock turn mid-flight—each individual responding to invisible cues, yet the whole moving as one. That coherence-in-chaos is what distinguishes rich ensemble storytelling from linear drama.

Ultimately, network effects remind us that no character exists in isolation. Every choice radiates outward, reshaping others' fates in ways unseen. In that sense, ensemble fiction mirrors the real world: we are all each other's consequences. The writer who understands this truth crafts not just stories but ecosystems— worlds where relationships generate motion, triangles create compression, and networks amplify it into symphony. When the last page turns, the reader doesn't remember just what happened. They remember how everyone moved—together, apart, across the geometry of feeling that defines every great story.

Chapter 5 — Plot as Decisions: Choice Architecture

A plot is a ledger of irreversible choices. Every scene, every act, every heartbeat of narrative tension comes down to this: someone wants something, risks something, and decides—rightly or wrongly—what to do next. The architecture of story is not built on coincidence or event but on causality, on the way human beings create their own momentum through decision. A coin toss may begin a story, but a choice sustains it. Without decision, the plot drifts like debris in current. With it, every action becomes a ripple that reshapes the water.

5.1 Causal Chains Over Coincidence

Coincidence is the sugar rush of storytelling—it offers instant excitement but fades quickly, leaving no nourishment behind. It might start the engine (two strangers meet on a delayed flight), but from that point on, causality must take the wheel. Readers trust stories where effects feel earned. They may forgive one lightning strike of luck, but they will not follow a protagonist whose life unfolds through convenient timing. A story becomes compelling not because things happen, but because things *happen because.*

The foundation of causal plotting lies in understanding that every scene is a **decision fork**. A character enters a situation with a goal, encounters resistance, and must choose a response. That choice alters their position in the world—sometimes imperceptibly, sometimes catastrophically. The accumulation of these alterations forms the plot's spine. If a scene begins and ends with the character unchanged, it's a placeholder, not a progression. You can measure the health of your story by tracing this pattern: choice → consequence → new problem → next choice.

It helps to think of plot not as a line but as a chain. Each link depends on the one before it. Remove a link, and the chain breaks. If you can shuffle scenes without the story losing coherence, your causal logic is weak. Revision begins with diagnosis: does each event grow from what precedes it? Does the protagonist's decision in Scene 5 create the conditions for Scene 6? If not, the story is relying on coincidence, not causation. The repair process isn't to add more action—it's to expose the decision that should have been there all along.

Causality gives story moral gravity. It teaches readers that choices have weight. A coincidence might amuse them, but a consequence moves them, because it mirrors the architecture of real life: every gain leaves a scar, every shortcut leaves a debt. When readers sense that a protagonist's actions carry inevitable repercussions, they invest emotionally. They start asking, *What will this cost?* And that question is the engine of suspense.

To build these decision forks consciously, begin by clarifying what each scene's **goal** truly is. Most writers mistake logistics for goals. "Break into the building" is an activity, not a goal. The real goal is what the activity accomplishes—"find proof to exonerate my brother." Once you've identified that goal, structure the scene so that the character must make a moral or strategic choice to pursue it. The choice doesn't need to be grand; even a small decision ("go alone or ask for help?") creates direction. What matters is that the decision has *visible stakes*—something to lose, something to gain, and something to change.

Ending a scene on summary—on a reflection, a restatement, or a pause—kills momentum. Ending on **changed state**—a shift in information, leverage, or relationship—propels the narrative forward. If a detective learns nothing new, you haven't advanced the story. But if she learns the wrong thing and acts on it, you've deepened the plot through consequence. Mistakes make better engines than victories because they multiply future decisions.

This idea of **causal integrity** applies even to stories that appear episodic or lyrical. In *The Great Gatsby*, every party scene is built around choices—Nick's choice to observe rather than intervene, Gatsby's choice to chase illusion over truth, Daisy's choice to retreat into comfort. The glitter may distract, but the chain beneath is forged of decisions that bind each glittering episode to the next. When Gatsby takes the blame for Daisy's accident, it's not coincidence that kills him; it's the inevitable extension of the loyalty he chose.

Causality doesn't mean predictability. The best stories obey internal logic while defying surface expectation. The reader shouldn't see what comes next, but when it arrives, it should feel like the only thing that could have happened. That's the paradox of good plotting: surprise that feels inevitable. The surprise comes from the character's psychology; the inevitability comes from the laws of cause and effect. When choice drives the plot, twist and truth become indistinguishable.

To stress-test your narrative, conduct a **post-mortem** on each major turning point. Ask: *What choice produced this outcome?* If you can't name one, you've probably relied on coincidence or authorial manipulation. A sudden car crash that removes a problem may thrill momentarily but erodes trust. A character deciding to drive recklessly out of anger before that crash? That restores causality and meaning. The difference is agency. The reader forgives disaster when it grows from emotion, not convenience.

Causality also demands **proportionate consequence**. Small choices can have large outcomes, but the emotional logic must balance. If a minor fib destroys a marriage, you need to show how that relationship was already under strain. If a single text message topples a government, you must build the groundwork of vulnerability beforehand. Proportion is what separates the inevitable from the arbitrary.

In ensemble stories, causal chains weave together like circuits. Each character's decision sends current through the system, illuminating different parts of the narrative. The intersection points—where one character's choice becomes another's crisis—create the illusion of complexity. But the mechanics are simple: everyone acts according to their wants and fears, and their choices collide. The result is plot.

Coincidence can still exist in stories, but it should work **against**, not **for**, the protagonist. A random misfortune reveals character by forcing improvisation; a random windfall merely delays consequence. When luck intervenes unfavorably, it strengthens causality by compelling new choices. When luck saves, it severs the chain. This distinction explains why readers will accept tragedy from fate but not victory from miracle. One honors struggle; the other cancels it.

The deepest form of causal storytelling is recursive: decisions don't just change events—they change the decision-maker. Each new consequence modifies the protagonist's understanding, reshaping future choices. This creates a self-learning system. The story's plot becomes its character arc. By the final act, the protagonist faces a decision that echoes the first but under transformed conditions. The symmetry reveals growth: what was once impossible is now necessary. That's narrative catharsis—a choice made with full knowledge of cost.

Writers often mistake causality for plot rigidity, fearing it will limit surprise. In truth, it liberates invention. Once you know the logical consequence of a decision, you can play within it—

exploring irony, misunderstanding, or unintended results. The story becomes not about controlling outcome but observing fallout. Like physics, causality gives freedom by defining rules. You can bend them but not break them.

Even nonlinear narratives depend on causal coherence. Time may loop, fragment, or reverse, but emotional cause and effect must remain legible. In *Arrival*, the protagonist's temporal perception is fractured, yet every action obeys emotional logic—love leads to sacrifice, knowledge leads to acceptance. If the story were shuffled arbitrarily, it would collapse. It's not chronology that creates structure; it's the causal bond between human motives and their consequences.

To ensure that bond survives revision, trace your protagonist's decision trail from first page to last. Remove any moment that exists solely to explain, decorate, or delay. Every scene should either introduce a choice, depict it, or reveal its cost. When you map your draft this way, you'll see where causality thins—the "soft joints" where coincidence sneaks in. Strengthen them by asking what human impulse could make the same thing happen. Replace accident with intention. Replace convenience with consequence.

Ultimately, causal storytelling respects both reader and character. It says: the world of this story obeys rules, and choices matter. It reflects the moral architecture of reality itself. We live in a universe where every decision—who to trust, what to reveal, when to act—echoes forward in ways we can't predict. Fiction, when built on causality, doesn't imitate life; it clarifies it. It takes the chaos of chance and filters it through meaning.

A well-constructed plot is not a series of events but a chain reaction of accountability. Each link gleams because it was forged by choice. When readers reach the final page and feel both satisfaction and inevitability, it's not because they've witnessed spectacle—it's because they've witnessed justice, the quiet justice of cause and effect. That's the essence of choice architecture: a story world where decisions leave fingerprints, and every consequence—whether triumph or ruin—bears the unmistakable shape of human will.

5.2 Stakes & Risk Ladders

Every choice only matters as much as it risks to lose. Without stakes, decisions are empty gestures—like gambling with counterfeit chips. The tension that drives plot does not arise from motion or spectacle but from consequence: the fear that one choice might destroy something irreplaceable. The artistry of plotting, then, lies in **escalating stakes** with deliberate precision—not through explosions or grand gestures, but through the tightening of invisible threads. The reader should feel a rising constriction in the chest, the sense that each move forward eliminates one more way back.

To construct this progression, think in terms of a **stakes matrix**—four interwoven layers that climb in intensity: personal, relational, public, and existential. Each layer draws power from the one below it. The personal stakes begin with self—what the character wants or fears losing. The relational tier amplifies it through the lens of connection—how the decision will affect the people they love, depend on, or betray. The public tier widens scope—how the decision reverberates through community, reputation, or power. Finally, the existential tier asks what happens to the character's very identity or belief system if the decision fails. A mature plot escalates across these layers, not just along one. The movement from private to cosmic gives the story both intimacy and weight.

A crime novel, for example, might begin with a detective's professional goal (personal) to solve a case, rise into conflict with a partner (relational) over how far they'll bend the rules, spiral into a scandal that jeopardizes public trust (public), and culminate in a moral crisis where the detective questions whether truth itself has value (existential). Each rung of the ladder inherits pressure from the one below, creating exponential intensity. The story ceases to be about a case and becomes about the meaning of integrity.

Escalation, however, isn't merely stacking larger consequences. It's removing safety nets one by one until the protagonist's margin for error disappears. A character can endure enormous danger if they feel some control—a weapon, an ally, a plausible excuse. The writer's job is to strip away those buffers. Each removal sharpens decision-making. When time runs out, when support vanishes, when even rationalization fails, the character must act from essence, not strategy. Those are the moments readers remember—the ones that expose not what a person *plans* to be, but what they *are*.

One of the most effective forms of escalation is the **erasure of time**. Limitations on duration make choices irreversible. A rescue mission with hours left invites confidence; with minutes left, it invites revelation. Compressing time transforms even small stakes into urgent ones. The ticking clock doesn't need to be literal; it can be emotional—a dying parent waiting for truth, a friend about to walk away, a secret that can't stay buried. The longer a character delays, the narrower the corridor becomes, until inaction itself becomes fatal.

But the ladder of risk is not purely external. Some of the most devastating consequences unfold in shadow—**invisible costs** that corrode identity or trust even when the protagonist "succeeds." These shadow costs are where emotional realism lives. The hero wins the trial but loses faith in justice. The activist saves the cause but sacrifices intimacy. The mother protects her child but teaches fear instead of strength. Such outcomes echo long after the plot resolves because they challenge the assumption that survival equals victory. Shadow costs ensure that progress always feels bittersweet, that the triumph of one value devours another.

Psychologically, shadow costs also reveal a deeper paradox: every decision that strengthens the Mask (from Chapter 3) weakens the self beneath it. When a character repeatedly chooses control over vulnerability, or expedience over honesty, they survive tactically but decay spiritually. By the climax, their external success may be indistinguishable from internal defeat. That friction between winning and becoming unrecognizable is the hallmark of sophisticated plotting. Readers sense that the stakes aren't just about what happens—they're about who remains afterward.

Effective escalation also depends on rhythm. Constant peril numbs; too little, and tension evaporates. The key is variation—oscillation between reprieve and crisis, like breathing. Each lull should introduce a new dimension of risk, not merely respite. A quiet dinner scene after chaos may feel safe until a single line of dialogue redefines everything—"You lied about where you were that night." Now emotional danger replaces physical. This pattern of alternating intensities creates narrative heartbeat.

Writers often mistake escalation for addition—more enemies, higher explosions, louder music. True escalation subtracts rather than adds. It confines. It isolates. It narrows options until each choice cuts closer to bone. When the audience realizes the protagonist has no safe option left—that every path demands self-betrayal or sacrifice—they experience catharsis. The choice that follows becomes mythic because it's paid for with identity.

The most powerful plots therefore operate like pressure chambers. The walls—time, allies, self-justification—slowly close in. At the start, the protagonist still believes they can outthink the problem. By the midpoint, strategy has failed; only belief remains. By the climax, even belief must be tested. The last rung of the stakes ladder isn't about survival at all—it's about what the character chooses to preserve when nothing else is left. Will they trade love for truth? Safety for freedom? Life for meaning? The answer, whatever it is, defines both ending and theme.

5.3 Reversals & Revelations

If causality is the skeleton and stakes are the muscle, reversals are the heartbeat—the rhythmic contraction and release that keeps story alive. A reversal doesn't simply shock; it changes direction. It flips the polarity of the world so that what seemed secure becomes precarious, and what seemed peripheral becomes central. A revelation, by contrast, alters understanding. Together they turn linear narrative into spiral—each new truth forcing readers to reinterpret everything they thought they knew.

The golden rule of reversals is fairness. You can surprise readers, but you can't cheat them. Plant evidence honestly, then guide attention through misdirection, not deceit. The reader should realize, in retrospect, that all the clues were visible—the pattern hidden only by perspective. True misdirection relies on human bias: characters, like readers, prioritize the wrong details, ignore quiet warnings, mistake comfort for certainty. When the reversal lands, we don't feel tricked; we feel enlightened.

The cleanest reversals are those that rewire power, not merely information. Discovering that a character lied is minor; realizing that lie changes who holds leverage is major. When a servant turns out to have been observing the master all along, hierarchy collapses. When the protagonist's victory reveals itself as the antagonist's plan, the story's gravity reverses direction. Power realignment ripples outward—it changes relationships, motives, and stakes simultaneously.

Reversals should arise from **decision**, not coincidence. They must be earned through the logic of character. When a choice made in Act One returns in Act Three as unintended doom, the reversal feels both poetic and inevitable. This circular causality creates moral weight—the sense that fate is not random but self-inflicted. Greek tragedy understood this long before modern thrillers did: revelation hurts because it exposes what the hero themselves set in motion.

To deepen effect, structure major turns as **two-step reveals**. The first step delivers partial truth—something that feels complete enough to satisfy, yet leaves a faint itch of unease. The second step, often delayed, recontextualizes it entirely. For example, a protagonist might discover that her mentor falsified data to protect her. That's step one—a betrayal that changes the emotional field. Step two, much later, reveals the deeper reason: the data was falsified not for protection but to conceal the mentor's own crime. Now the betrayal expands into tragedy, reframing earlier sympathy as blindness. Each layer of truth changes the emotional color of every prior scene.

Revelations gain power when they require reinterpretation, not replacement. If new information invalidates everything before, the reader feels discarded; if it reframes what was already there, they feel rewarded. The difference lies in continuity. A masterful revelation doesn't say, *You were wrong to believe that.* It says, *You were right, but not enough.* That subtle upgrade from falsehood to complexity mirrors the way people experience truth in life—it unfolds, it accretes, it deepens.

To stage reversals effectively, calibrate timing and emotional contrast. The human mind registers shock most strongly when contradiction follows stability. A serene wedding interrupted by a confession; a moment of triumph cut short by betrayal. These juxtapositions amplify impact because they challenge expectation at its peak. But restraint is key: one great reversal outweighs five minor stunts. The purpose is not to twist for novelty but to evolve understanding.

Reversals can also occur internally. The protagonist discovers that their enemy mirrors their own motives, or that their victory ensures another's ruin. These internal revelations shift emotional geometry without altering external events. They are quieter but often more profound. The story's surface remains unchanged, yet its meaning inverts. Such turns resonate because they strike not at circumstance but at perception—the recognition that self and world were misaligned all along.

Perhaps the most overlooked aspect of revelation is aftermath. A twist has no value unless it transforms behavior. Once truth arrives, characters must make new decisions under the weight of that knowledge. The revelation becomes fuel for further causality. If no new choice follows, the story stalls. In other words, the reveal is never an endpoint—it's an ignition.

The ethical dimension of reversals lies in empathy. Each new understanding invites the reader to expand compassion. We thought we knew the villain; now we glimpse their wound. We thought we understood the hero's motive; now we see its selfish core. Reversal of sympathy is the highest form of revelation because it forces moral participation. The reader must renegotiate their allegiance, just as the characters must renegotiate theirs.

When done well, the final revelation doesn't just answer mystery—it fuses emotion and logic into one inevitable image. The audience realizes that everything—every earlier choice, every overlooked detail—was always converging here. It's the moment of *of course* following *no way*. That paradox is the hallmark of earned surprise.

By the end of a causally driven story, the reader can trace the full circuit: choices built consequences, stakes magnified cost, reversals illuminated hidden truth. The plot's final revelation is therefore not just factual—it's philosophical. It reveals the governing law of this world, the moral gravity under which every decision fell. When the reader closes the book, what lingers isn't shock but recognition: that life, like fiction, is a series of decisions paid for in understanding. The story ends not when everything is known, but when there are no more choices left to make.

Chapter 6 — Structures to Steal (and Bend)

Structure is scaffold, not prison. The most inventive writers understand that frameworks exist not to constrain creativity but to give it form—like the invisible armature beneath a sculpture that lets clay hold its shape. To reject structure entirely is to mistake chaos for freedom; to worship it blindly is to trade vitality for obedience. True mastery lies in knowing the bones well enough to rearrange them. You steal what works, bend what doesn't, and let the architecture disappear beneath the illusion of natural motion. Readers should never notice your structure; they should feel it the way a body feels its skeleton—essential, invisible, supporting everything else.

6.1 Four Flexible Frameworks

Every story, whether epic or intimate, depends on rhythm—moments of tension and release, promise and payoff. Structure is simply the map of that rhythm. Yet there's no single map that fits every terrain. Different stories breathe in different tempos, and knowing multiple frameworks lets you match architecture to intention. Among the many models available, four have endured not as formulas but as repeatable thought experiments: the **Fichtean Curve**, the **Seven Point Arc**, the **Kishōtenketsu**, and the **Heist/Caper Model**. Each carries its own philosophy of momentum, and each can be borrowed, broken, or blended to suit the tone you need.

The **Fichtean Curve** is perhaps the most kinetic of the four—a structure designed for propulsion. Imagine the story not as a series of plateaus but as a continuous incline, each event feeding directly into the next crisis. The protagonist is almost never at rest. There are no early expositions, no leisurely openings; conflict erupts by paragraph two. Every apparent solution spawns a new problem, tightening the noose of consequence until the character either transforms or breaks. It's a pressure cooker model, ideal for thrillers, survival stories, or any narrative where momentum substitutes for oxygen.

The power of the Fichtean Curve lies in its relentless chaining of cause and effect. It demands compression: every beat is both reaction and setup. When used well, it creates the sensation of inevitability—readers turning pages not because they're curious about what happens next, but because they *must* see what the last decision unleashes. Yet its danger is fatigue. Without modulation, tension plateaus into numbness. The trick is micro-variation: alternating physical crisis with moral or psychological ones. The external fire keeps burning, but the fuel changes form.

Writers can also bend the Fichtean shape by reversing its logic. Instead of escalation through action, you can escalate through *reduction*—each scene smaller, quieter, closer to silence, as in a chamber play or psychological dissection. The curve still climbs, but the energy inverts: pressure turns inward instead of outward. This inversion works beautifully for stories of introspection, where the "crisis" is realization rather than event.

If the Fichtean model is a climb, the **Seven Point Structure** is a map with landmarks—clear, evenly spaced waypoints that guide character and theme with precision. It's the engineer's approach to narrative: organized, logical, and deeply humane. The seven points—hook, first plot turn, midpoint, pinch points, climax, resolution—form a symmetrical pattern reminiscent of a musical composition. You begin by showing what's missing, then oscillate between setbacks and discoveries until the final resolution delivers not surprise but inevitability.

This model's strength is its adaptability. You can shrink it to a short story or expand it to a trilogy. Because it emphasizes turning points rather than sheer velocity, it's perfect for character-centric tales where emotional calibration matters more than spectacle. A Seven Point story feels satisfying because it tracks growth as well as motion. Each milestone represents not just what happens, but what the protagonist *understands* now that they didn't before.

To keep the Seven Point from becoming mechanical, remember that structure exists to trace emotional logic, not page count. A midpoint doesn't mean "halfway through the book"—it means "halfway through understanding." The beauty of this model is how easily it accommodates moral geometry. You can twist it into tragedy by flipping polarity—what was gained becomes lost, what was found becomes illusion. Or you can reframe it cyclically: the resolution mirrors the hook, but with awareness transformed. Used flexibly, it creates stories that feel architecturally sound without ever showing the beams.

Then comes **Kishōtenketsu**, the quiet radical from the East. Originating in Japanese and Chinese narrative traditions, it offers an antidote to the Western obsession with conflict. Kishōtenketsu unfolds in four stages—introduction (ki), development (shō), twist (ten), and conclusion (ketsu)—but the twist is not born of opposition. It's born of contrast. Instead of collision, the story pivots. A new perspective enters, recontextualizing what came before. The pleasure lies not in resolution but in juxtaposition, in the moment when two seemingly unrelated threads reveal resonance.

This structure excels in discovery-based narratives, essays, travelogues, or slice-of-life fiction where tension grows through observation. It invites curiosity instead of anxiety. A painter studies light, then shadow, then realizes both are facets of the same subject. A character's daily routine acquires meaning only when interrupted by an image or idea that reframes it. The Kishōtenketsu allows revelation without destruction—it says, "See this differently," rather than "Defeat this enemy."

Western writers can learn from its restraint. Too often, we mistake drama for shouting. Kishōtenketsu proves that revelation can emerge from harmony as much as discord. When adapted into other genres, it adds depth by introducing thematic or tonal pivots: the detective story that becomes memoir halfway through, the love story that turns into meditation on aging. The plot doesn't escalate; it metamorphoses.

Finally, there's the **Heist/Caper Model**, storytelling as orchestration. Where other structures track an individual's growth, the heist tracks collective choreography: assemble the team, plan the operation, execute, and deal with fallout. It's inherently modular—each section can flex, repeat, or fold back on itself depending on how much suspense you need. What makes this structure so enduring isn't theft; it's *process*. Readers and viewers alike are addicted to competence—the pleasure of watching chaos resolved through mastery, until mastery itself unravels.

The elegance of the heist lies in its symmetry of illusion. The plan we see early on is rarely the real plan. Each phase—recruitment, rehearsal, execution—contains seeds of betrayal or adaptation. The story becomes a study in systems thinking: how individuals merge into machine, how trust becomes the most fragile currency. The "fallout" phase, where the team fractures under pressure, often delivers the story's deepest emotional beats. After the score comes reckoning. After competence comes conscience.

Writers can transpose this model beyond crime. Any collaborative enterprise—scientific discovery, political campaign, startup launch—can borrow the heist's modular rhythm. The key is coordination under time pressure followed by entropy. The reader watches as synergy peaks, then collapses. In comedy, the fallout is absurdity; in tragedy, guilt. What endures is the satisfaction of structure: the sense that each phase logically transforms into the next.

Blending these frameworks often yields the richest results. You might run a heist's four-act architecture through a Fichtean lens to maintain momentum, or lace a Seven Point character arc into a Kishōtenketsu tonal pivot. Hybridization reflects the evolution of storytelling itself. As audiences grow more literate in form, they crave both recognition and novelty—the comfort of familiar rhythm with the thrill of broken expectation.

Still, to bend structure effectively, you must internalize it first. Study it until instinct replaces analysis. Only then can you manipulate beats without the seams showing. Think of structure as grammar: you learn rules to break them elegantly. An unstructured story reads like a conversation without punctuation—energetic but exhausting. A structured one breathes; it gives the reader space to anticipate, to feel contrast, to sense that time itself has shape.

When you steal a framework, do it with reverence and mischief. Reverence for the centuries of narrative engineering that preceded you; mischief for the possibilities still untested. A structure is a question, not an answer. What happens if the midpoint comes first? What if the "team" in your heist never meets? What if the Kishōtenketsu's twist is moral instead of narrative? Every story inherits a skeleton; originality lies in how you teach it to dance.

Ultimately, all structures serve one truth: human beings crave pattern. We want to believe that meaning can be organized, that chaos can resolve into shape. That's why readers will follow a curve, a sequence, a pivot, a plan—they want to feel time crystallize into significance. But within that order, they also want surprise, friction, life. The scaffolding should vanish beneath motion, leaving only rhythm, pulse, and breath. When you master structure, you no longer build cages for your stories. You build wings sturdy enough to let them fly.

6.2 Modular Story Tiles

Stories are often built like rivers—flowing, continuous, each event pouring into the next—but the truth is that many of the most memorable narratives are mosaics. They are constructed from modular units, self-contained yet interdependent, each functioning as a miniature ecosystem of tension, change, and release. I call these **story tiles**—discrete narrative chambers that can stand alone yet, when arranged, create a greater design. Understanding how to craft and link these tiles allows you to control pacing, emotional rhythm, and variety. Modular construction is not fragmentation; it's choreography. Each module pulses with its own internal logic before surrendering to the whole.

The most recognizable of these units is the **setpiece tile**. A setpiece isn't just spectacle; it's structure condensed into a single dramatic encounter. Think of it as a self-contained short story embedded within the novel—a sequence governed by clear rules, a visible goal, and an escalating scorecard. The audience should understand what constitutes success and failure, even if the characters themselves do not. A courtroom scene, a duel, a negotiation, a dinner party—all qualify when they contain their own arc: preparation, confrontation, reversal, and aftermath.

Setpieces thrive on constraint. The tension arises from watching characters operate inside a defined system of rules, testing ingenuity under pressure. In a chase, the geography becomes the rulebook; in a trial, it's procedure; in an emotional confrontation, it's decorum. The scoreboard is what keeps us watching. We know when the hero is gaining ground or losing it. Every beat moves a visible counter, so the audience stays oriented amid chaos. When the setpiece ends, it leaves a measurable change in status—power, knowledge, or intimacy—feeding back into the broader narrative.

Writers sometimes confuse setpieces with filler, mistaking them for decorative "big moments." In truth, they are engines. A well-designed tile compresses multiple story functions: advancing plot, revealing character, dramatizing theme. A single argument over dinner might expose betrayal, flip alliances, and foreshadow tragedy. Because it contains its own rise and fall, the setpiece offers satisfying closure within momentum—a miniature symphony nested inside the larger score.

The opposite of expansiveness is confinement, and the **bottle chapter** represents its purest form. Borrowed from television jargon ("bottle episodes"), this type of story tile traps the characters in one location or situation—often with no external action to escape the tension. The limits become the drama. In a bottle chapter, space contracts so that psychology expands. Confined settings strip away distraction, forcing characters to confront what they've avoided.

A bottle chapter might take place in a stuck elevator, a cabin during a storm, a jury room, or a quarantine ward. What matters isn't the setting itself but the pressure of enclosure. Without escape routes, the emotional temperature rises naturally. Secrets surface, relationships fracture or heal, truths are confessed because silence becomes unbearable. These chapters often serve as emotional recalibration points within a novel, deepening interior stakes before the next external act. They function as crucibles—melting, forging, purifying.

Technically, bottle chapters also provide pacing relief. After several high-momentum tiles, a confined scene slows tempo without losing tension. The story breathes differently; instead of sprinting forward, it burns inward. For the reader, this contrast is essential. It creates texture—a shift from kinetic energy to psychological gravity. The writer gains a chance to let dialogue, memory, and subtext carry the load.

However, a bottle chapter demands precision. Without movement, every line must earn its place. The writer's challenge is to orchestrate escalation inside stillness: new emotional layers must unfold even when geography doesn't. One technique is to assign each participant a hidden agenda that slowly leaks out under pressure, turning the room into an arena of unspoken war. When handled with discipline, a bottle chapter can feel more explosive than any car chase.

The third major tile, the **frame story**, introduces the dimension of time and perception. It's not just a device—it's a philosophical stance. The outer frame, often a narrator or context in which the central story is told, acts as a mirror. It questions, reinterprets, or distorts the inner narrative, creating dialogue between layers. The classic example is *The Arabian Nights*, where Scheherazade's storytelling becomes both survival strategy and meditation on power. But framing isn't confined to folklore. Modern works like *The Princess Bride* or *Heart of Darkness* employ frames to interrogate the act of storytelling itself—who tells the story, who controls meaning, what is remembered versus what is true.

A good frame story doesn't simply bookend the narrative; it shapes how we read it. The outer narrator's bias or limitation infuses the inner tale with irony. A story told by an aging soldier about his youthful bravery reads differently than if the events were presented directly. The frame establishes distance, and with distance comes theme—memory, revision, regret. You can even reverse the hierarchy, letting the inner tale comment on the outer frame. The listener changes the teller; the teller rewrites the story mid-course. This interplay of voices builds a meta-layer of awareness, inviting readers to become interpreters rather than consumers.

Framing also allows you to play with temporal depth. A modern researcher uncovering a lost journal, a grandparent recounting an event long past, a robot reconstructing a vanished civilization—all use the frame to contrast eras and moral assumptions. The outer and inner stories illuminate each other like faces on opposite sides of glass. What we think we know about one shifts when we glimpse the other.

The most successful modular novels weave all three tiles—setpiece, bottle, and frame—into an ecosystem of scale and contrast. The setpiece gives kinetic release, the bottle chapter delivers intimacy, and the frame provides reflection. Together they create a rhythm of expansion and contraction, action and contemplation. Modular architecture doesn't fragment narrative—it grants it elasticity. It gives the reader multiple levels of immersion: surface thrill, emotional depth, and philosophical echo.

To master this modular approach, train yourself to see each chapter as a cell within an organism. It must metabolize its own oxygen—begin, intensify, conclude—while contributing to the larger heartbeat. When one tile weakens, the whole structure limps. But when each functions with internal coherence, the story becomes fractal: each part mirrors the whole in miniature.

6.3 Braids & Nested Loops

If modular tiles give structure density, **braids and nested loops** give it motion—rhythmic, interlocking, and self-renewing.

Whereas a linear story traces a single thread from start to finish, a braided narrative intertwines multiple threads, each with its own color, tempo, and emotional logic. The beauty of this design lies in contrast: different arcs rubbing against each other, generating texture and resonance. The reader experiences not one continuous melody but polyphony.

A braid typically interleaves two or more storylines—say, a quest, a romance, and a mystery. Each strand develops independently but intersects at emotional or thematic nodes. The quest provides propulsion, the romance offers vulnerability, and the mystery adds suspense. Together they form harmonic rhythm. The challenge is balance: no strand should dominate for too long, or the braid unravels. Each must yield spotlight and regain it in turn, like dancers passing partners.

Crafting a braid requires attention to **tempo**. The A-line may move fast, full of action and external stakes; the B-line slower, meditative; the C-line perhaps lyrical or intellectual. Alternating these tempos prevents reader fatigue and multiplies engagement. When an intense sequence ends, cutting to a quieter subplot doesn't weaken tension—it sustains curiosity by shifting frequency. The reader's nervous system recalibrates, ready for the next surge.

The **nested loop**, by contrast, operates like a spiral rather than a weave. It's the art of placing stories within stories, promises within promises, each enclosed by another layer. A mystery hides inside a quest; within that quest lies a test of love; within that test, a secret about selfhood. Each loop carries its own mini-arc, but the completion of one loop unlocks the next, pulling the reader deeper. The pleasure comes from recursion—the sense that meaning keeps unfolding inward, like a Russian doll or a sequence of dreams.

The power of nesting is that it sustains curiosity indefinitely. Every time one question resolves, another awakens, slightly closer to the core. The outer loops provide momentum; the inner ones provide revelation. Readers don't simply want answers—they want patterns that promise answers. Nested structures deliver this continuously. The best example is found in stories where myth and memory overlap—one tale explaining another, then dissolving back into it. The narrative becomes less a line and more an echo chamber, where each repetition reveals a new frequency.

Managing these braids and loops demands visual thinking. Many writers literally color-code their outlines—one shade per strand—to monitor distribution. This isn't bureaucracy; it's musical notation. You're ensuring that emotional and thematic tones alternate in harmony. If one color overshadows others for too long, imbalance sets in: too much quest and the story loses tenderness; too much romance and it loses urgency. Balance doesn't mean equality—it means rhythm, the pulse of variation.

But the deeper secret to effective braiding lies in *convergence*. Distinct threads must ultimately inform one another, even if they never literally meet. The romance may resolve the mystery's emotional question; the quest may dramatize the moral lesson of the love story. When separate arcs illuminate a shared theme from different angles, the reader feels synthesis—a click of unity disguised as surprise. The whole becomes more than its parts.

Nested loops also mirror how human understanding unfolds. We rarely grasp truth in a straight line; we circle it, revisiting from new vantage points. Each return to the loop's center deepens insight. This pattern invites readers to experience discovery alongside characters. The structure itself becomes metaphor: knowledge as recursion, meaning as return.

You can use braids and loops to control *information flow*. By alternating strands, you manipulate suspense through strategic withholding. Reveal a clue in the mystery thread, then cut to the romance before it's explained. The reader reads faster, propelled by the unfinished pattern. The shift also refreshes empathy; tension in one line intensifies investment in another. This alternation mimics consciousness itself—our minds rarely focus on one drama at a time.

A mature braid also leverages asymmetry. Some strands resolve early, others late, some not at all. This variation mirrors life's incompleteness and gives texture to closure. When the final loop snaps shut—when the outermost layer resolves and the innermost truth surfaces—the reader feels both release and echo, as though hearing the last note of a chord fade into silence.

Braiding isn't merely technique; it's worldview. It asserts that no single perspective holds the whole truth, that meaning arises through intersection. In this way, the structure becomes theme: plurality, complexity, interdependence. Nested loops take this further by making knowledge itself the journey—every revelation provisional, every ending a doorway.

When you weave these methods—modular tiles, braids, and loops—you gain control over narrative texture. You can pace emotion like a composer modulates tempo, build resonance across chapters, and sustain curiosity without resorting to gimmick. Each device, when used with intention, teaches the reader how to listen to your story's particular rhythm.

Ultimately, structure is not about rules but relationships— between events, between perspectives, between meanings. A braided, modular, nested narrative reflects how we actually experience existence: in fragments that cohere, in stories that overlap, in circles that never quite close but keep turning, alive.

Chapter 7 — Time & Pacing: Narrative Clocks

Readers feel time moving even when nothing explodes. The pulse of a story is not measured in car chases or countdowns but in perception—how the reader experiences change, consequence, and anticipation across pages. Pacing is the invisible metronome of narrative, the rhythm that tells us when to lean forward and when to breathe. It determines whether a story feels inevitable or indulgent, spare or swollen. When pacing falters, even the most beautiful sentences feel stagnant; when it works, even silence vibrates with tension. Writers often mistake pace for speed, but the truer distinction is between attention and drift. You're not trying to go fast—you're trying to keep the reader's mind engaged in motion.

7.1 Compression vs. Dilation

Mastering time in fiction begins with knowing when to compress and when to dilate. The rhythm of storytelling depends on this alternation—the way narrative breathes by tightening and releasing its grip on time. Compression collapses the uneventful, the repetitive, the transitional; dilation expands the charged moment, the hinge where meaning crystallizes. To control time is to control focus, and focus is the essence of storytelling.

Compression is the art of invisibility. It's what allows months, years, even decades to vanish between paragraphs without confusion. A writer compresses time through summary—narrative language that gathers experience into gesture, condensing multiple actions or impressions into a single sentence. "For three years she worked, slept little, and learned not to look anyone in the eye." In one stroke, entire seasons disappear, leaving behind residue—habit, fatigue, change. The reader doesn't feel cheated because compression imitates memory; we remember not every day but the feeling of accumulation.

Compression works best when the skipped material lacks inflection. Inflection points are the seams where change happens, where decisions alter direction. These you dramatize; everything else you distill. The reader's mind accepts compression as natural because it mirrors how consciousness moves—jumping from one relevant instant to another, ignoring the static between. The key is to keep the emotional current intact. Summary must still convey transformation, however swiftly. It's not absence of motion but acceleration through essentials.

Within scenes, micro compression creates efficiency without numbness. You can condense minutes into moments by selecting details that imply duration. "The coffee went cold between them" suggests an hour of silence without narrating every minute. Micro summaries also let you accelerate transitions inside continuous action. Instead of chronicling every footstep through a city, you might write, "They wandered through the market's chaos until fatigue blurred the colors." The sentence becomes a bridge— compression that preserves mood.

Too much compression, however, risks detachment. When time collapses entirely, readers lose the sensory thread that anchors them to the moment. That's where dilation restores balance. If compression is memory, dilation is presence—the magnification of perception until a single heartbeat occupies a page. Dilation happens when you slow language to match intensity, when you let consciousness linger on detail because detail has become meaning.

Imagine a character reaching for a door handle before a life-changing revelation. The act takes seconds, yet you might stretch it across paragraphs: the tremor in the wrist, the temperature of the brass, the sound of wind in the corridor. Each observation suspends time, allowing emotion to bloom in microscopic focus. Dilation transforms action into experience. The reader knows the door will open, but they feel the weight of waiting—an inner physics of hesitation and fear.

The trick lies in modulation. A story written entirely in dilation suffocates; one built only on compression feels skeletal. The narrative clock must tick at variable speeds, its tempo adjusted to emotional gravity. Large-scale time (months, years) can move briskly while small-scale time (a glance, a realization) slows to near stillness. The alternation itself generates rhythm. Fast passages create hunger for pause; slow passages gain tension from the promise of acceleration.

One of the most effective tools for managing this rhythm is **temporal signaling**—anchoring the reader in time through concrete markers. These markers need not be numerical ("three days later"); they can be sensory: the angle of light, the state of the sky, the tone of a voice. When readers feel disoriented, it's rarely because chronology is unclear—it's because sensory continuity has broken. A simple shift in temperature or sound can signal elapsed time more vividly than any date stamp. "The cicadas had gone quiet since morning." Instantly, we know a day has passed, and with it, mood.

Temporal signals also govern emotional pacing. Dawn, dusk, meal times, weather—all carry psychological resonance. Dawn feels like potential; dusk feels like closure. A sudden rain can compress hours of conversation into intimacy; a long dry season can stretch longing across chapters. Writers who handle time masterfully understand that chronology is inseparable from atmosphere. Time moves not just forward but inward, shaping tone and thought.

The greatest storytellers manipulate time without readers noticing. Virginia Woolf can make a dinner last a lifetime and a lifetime feel like a dinner. Tolstoy expands seconds of battle into metaphysical eternity, while Hemingway can kill years between sentences. Their secret isn't magic—it's calibration. They adjust narrative aperture the way a cinematographer adjusts lens width. When emotion deepens, they zoom in; when momentum demands, they pull back.

To practice this craft, try rewriting a scene twice: once as summary, once as slow-motion. In the summary version, condense the scene to ten lines. In the slow-motion version, stretch a single gesture to ten pages. Then hybridize them. The result will teach you how pace alters perception. The same event can feel tragic or trivial depending on how long you make the reader inhabit it.

Compression also carries thematic implications. When a story repeatedly skips time, it implies alienation—a life blurred by repetition or numbness. The act of elision becomes commentary. Conversely, dilation signals reverence or trauma. When time stalls, it's often because consciousness refuses to move on. This psychological rhythm mirrors grief, passion, or awe. Thus, pacing is not only structural but emotional—the tempo of feeling itself.

Writers often underestimate the power of transition phrases to manage tempo. Simple cues—"That night," "In the weeks that followed," "By winter"—do more than orient chronology; they act as breaths between heartbeats. They give readers permission to reset. Without these rests, even the fastest story feels static because the rhythm never changes. Motion depends on contrast: fast must follow slow, silence must follow noise.

Another way to control pacing is through syntax. Long, meandering sentences mimic thought and slow the pulse. Short ones quicken it. Varying these creates musicality. A sudden staccato line after a paragraph of lyric description can jolt the reader like a percussion strike. Conversely, an extended sentence after a flurry of short ones can stretch time, easing tension. Sentence rhythm, not just plot rhythm, dictates how time feels.

In revision, watch for passages where time feels flat—where neither compression nor dilation operates clearly. Flatness usually means indecision: the writer has described events without choosing whether they matter. Decide what kind of time each scene inhabits. If nothing changes, condense it; if everything changes, slow it down. Pacing is simply the discipline of prioritization—giving weight to transformation and brevity to maintenance.

Finally, remember that readers don't measure time by clocks but by *change*. Ten pages can feel like an instant if every paragraph alters perception. A single sentence can feel eternal if it suspends us in recognition. The writer's true clock is emotional consequence. When a story's internal time aligns with the reader's psychological time, you achieve narrative gravity—the sense that something larger than plot is ticking beneath the words.

To write time well is to conduct attention. You're not just deciding what happens next—you're deciding how long it takes for the reader to *feel* it. The story's hours, days, and years are raw material; pacing transforms them into music. Some beats must rush, some must linger, and between them lies the silence that makes the rhythm audible. Time is the medium through which meaning passes. Mastering compression and dilation means learning to sculpt that medium—to bend chronology until it breathes with the same irregular, irresistible rhythm as life itself.

7.2 The Three Clock Method

Every story operates on three overlapping systems of time: the time within the world, the time as the reader experiences it, and the time the writer spends creating it. These are the **Story Clock**, the **Reader Clock**, and the **Writer Clock**—three invisible gears that must mesh if the narrative is to run smoothly. When one slips, the illusion of momentum falters. The secret to pacing is not in choosing one clock to follow but in learning how to synchronize all three, allowing them to drive and counterbalance each other like hands on a dial.

The **Story Clock** governs diegetic time—the lived continuity of your fictional world. It is the spine that keeps chronology coherent: how long a journey takes, how many nights a character spends in recovery, how much time passes between an argument and its fallout. When the Story Clock loses accuracy, readers may not consciously notice, but they feel unease. A character who travels continents overnight or recovers from injury too quickly breaks suspension of disbelief. Conversely, a well-maintained Story Clock creates credibility even in the fantastic. You can bend physics, but you can't cheat perception; readers will accept magic faster than they will accept bad timing.

To master the Story Clock, you must become both architect and stage manager. Every scene exists in relationship to a larger temporal system: morning or night, before or after an event, within a week, a month, a season. Keeping a visible timeline—whether scribbled on a wall or charted digitally—prevents contradictions and highlights opportunities. Perhaps two subplots occur concurrently, creating irony. Perhaps a flashback interrupts a day that never resumes. The Story Clock doesn't demand rigid realism, but it does require rhythm. Fictional time can stretch or compress, yet transitions between these modes must feel intentional.

One of the most underappreciated functions of the Story Clock is *recovery time*. Too many narratives rush from crisis to crisis without letting bodies or emotions reset. A wound that heals overnight may seem convenient, but it drains tension; a grief that vanishes by the next chapter erases consequence. Recovery sequences, even brief ones, reassert realism and deepen empathy. They remind readers that time has weight. Similarly, travel scenes, when calibrated correctly, act as narrative metronomes—marking the distance between conflicts. The trick is not to dramatize the entire journey but to show evidence of passage: dust on boots, fatigue in dialogue, a landscape subtly altered by weather or season. These details make the Story Clock audible beneath the prose.

Parallel to the Story Clock runs the **Reader Clock**, the psychological tempo by which your audience experiences duration. It has little to do with diegetic time and everything to do with sensation. A story may cover years yet feel fast; another may describe an afternoon yet feel vast. The Reader Clock measures attention, not chronology. It ticks according to sentence length, paragraph density, white space, and scene rhythm. When the Reader Clock accelerates, pages turn almost involuntarily; when it slows, readers linger, absorbing atmosphere. A writer must learn to manipulate this tempo deliberately—speeding it when suspense demands, decelerating it when emotion or reflection must resonate.

Scene length acts as the primary lever of the Reader Clock. Short scenes deliver staccato energy, like quick camera cuts; long scenes immerse, building sustained tension or sensual texture. Neither is inherently superior—the craft lies in alternation. After a rapid sequence of brief chapters, a longer one feels monumental. After an extended scene of introspection, a sharp, decisive action shocks the senses. This modulation mirrors the body's need for contrast: tension and release, inhale and exhale.

White space is another crucial instrument. Paragraph breaks function as pauses in speech, giving the reader a breath before plunging on. Strategic use of short paragraphs can create acceleration by mimicking the pattern of quickened thought, while dense blocks of text slow reading and invite reflection. Even a single-line paragraph, isolated by blankness, can pulse like a drumbeat in the reader's mind. White space doesn't merely separate—it communicates silence, hesitation, or anticipation. When you control layout, you control the Reader Clock's heartbeat.

Clifflets—miniature hooks at scene or section ends—keep the Reader Clock ticking between chapters. They don't always require danger or revelation; sometimes a single unresolved emotional note suffices. The goal is to leave a micro-question hanging: What now? What next? By alternating closure and clifflet, you create momentum without resorting to artificial suspense. Readers should feel compelled forward because curiosity burns, not because they've been tricked into obligation.

Finally, there is the **Writer Clock**—the rhythm of your own creative process. This clock determines how effectively you can sustain the other two. Writing is physical labor, and pacing your sessions to match story intensity prevents burnout. The Writer Clock asks you to treat drafting as performance: sprints, rests, crescendos. During scenes of high tension, write fast, in bursts, letting energy carry the language. During contemplative scenes, slow your typing, listen to cadence, breathe with the character. The body's rhythm will often mirror the emotional rhythm of the story.

One valuable trick for maintaining the Writer Clock is to stop mid-line or mid-beat at the end of a session. This creates momentum for the next return. Starting from a cliffhanger of your own making eliminates the inertia of reentry. It's the same principle musicians use when rehearsing: always stop before the easy part. That way, the next practice begins with flow instead of friction.

Sprinting in short timed bursts—fifteen, twenty, forty minutes—also aligns your creative metabolism with story pulse. You write through fear, not around it, focusing on motion rather than judgment. The result is prose that carries kinetic residue. Later, during revision, you can recalibrate tempo objectively, layering structure over instinct.

The interaction of these three clocks creates harmony. The Story Clock ensures coherence, the Reader Clock ensures engagement, and the Writer Clock ensures sustainability. When they align, pacing feels inevitable. When they conflict, you can feel the dissonance instantly: a scene too short for the world's timeline, or prose too fast for its emotion. Like instruments in an orchestra, each must tune to the others. You can't rush the music of narrative without throwing it off-key.

7.3 Sentence & Paragraph Tempo

The micro level of pacing begins where syntax meets breath. Sentences are not neutral carriers of information; they are time in linguistic form. A short clause moves like a heartbeat, quick and decisive. A long, coiling sentence expands perception, asking the reader to inhabit thought. Mastering sentence and paragraph tempo means learning to play with linguistic rhythm so that meaning and music align.

Fast prose depends on concision—short clauses, concrete verbs, minimal modifiers. This doesn't mean abandoning beauty; it means locating it in precision rather than ornament. Action-driven sequences should read with the immediacy of muscle memory. Instead of "He quickly ran down the street," write "He sprinted." The verb itself carries velocity. Compression of syntax mirrors urgency in sensation. When sentences shorten, readers unconsciously increase eye movement; their bodies participate in speed.

Slow prose, on the other hand, invites expansion. Layered syntax allows contemplation; subordinate clauses mimic wandering thought. A moment of realization might demand a sentence that refuses to end, circling the insight until it ripens. Rhythm here mirrors consciousness: when we reflect, we linger. Dilation at the sentence level corresponds to dilation at the narrative level—the two are fractals of one another.

Paragraphs act as larger units of breath. Their boundaries control how readers experience time, emotion, and suspense. Breaking too often creates staccato rhythm—effective for tension but tiring if sustained. Allowing paragraphs to run long produces immersion, but too much density can smother momentum. Think of paragraphs as waveforms: rise, crest, and crash. Each should deliver a complete energy cycle before the next begins. When the rhythm aligns with emotional logic, the reader feels carried, not dragged.

White space functions as silence—the negative space where anticipation builds. A single blank line between paragraphs can suggest elapsed time or emotional distance. In a confrontation scene, a deliberate line break before a crucial response creates hesitation that feels alive. The reader inhales before the blow lands. This manipulation of space is as vital as any word choice. Pacing, at its finest, is choreography between language and pause.

Repetition devices like parallelism and anaphora add another rhythmic layer, creating waves within prose. Used sparingly, they generate hypnotic propulsion—the echo of incantation. "He waited for the train, waited for the night, waited for something to change." The rhythm accumulates pressure, transforming monotony into suspense. Overused, it dulls. The line between spell and sermon lies in variation. Always break the pattern before it becomes predictable; rhythm thrives on the tension between repetition and release.

Sound, too, affects tempo. Hard consonants snap like percussion; long vowels stretch like sustained notes. Read your sentences aloud to hear whether they rush or linger. Editing by ear often reveals pacing flaws invisible on the page. The eye may tolerate clutter; the ear demands proportion.

At the emotional level, tempo reflects psychology. A character in panic perceives fragments: clipped sentences, sensory bursts. A character in grief or wonder drifts into elongation. Aligning syntax with state of mind transforms prose into empathy. The reader doesn't just observe emotion—they feel its rhythm. This alignment between grammar and psyche is what turns description into experience.

Transitions between fast and slow passages must be fluid. Abrupt shifts jar unless anchored by sensory or tonal continuity. You can move from action to reflection by pivoting on an image: the smoke from an explosion turning into fog over a quiet field. The reader rides the metaphoric continuity across temporal change. Paragraph tempo, then, is not only about pacing but about coherence—ensuring that speed variations serve emotional evolution rather than randomness.

During revision, treat sentences like measures of music. Mark where tempo accelerates, where it drags, where silence could heighten tension. If a paragraph feels heavy, cut connective tissue; if it feels hollow, extend rhythm through echo or description. The goal isn't uniformity but pulse—a living fluctuation that mirrors the body's own patterns.

Ultimately, sentence and paragraph tempo are the smallest but most intimate instruments of narrative time. They operate beneath awareness, guiding heartbeat and breath as readers move through your world. Mastery of them means you no longer rely on plot to create pace; the language itself propels motion. When rhythm aligns with emotion, time becomes elastic. A page can hold an eternity, or an eternity can collapse into a line. The writer's task is to make both feel inevitable—to shape prose that breathes as naturally as the reader who follows it.

Chapter 8 — Point of View & Voice: Access and Attitude

Voice is attitude; point of view is access. Together they determine not only *what* a reader knows but *how* that knowledge feels. Point of view is the window—its size, shape, and tint—while voice is the light coming through it. A story's emotional temperature, its intimacy, its authority, all arise from this partnership. You can tell the same sequence of events through infinite lenses, yet each produces a different truth. The craft of fiction begins when you understand that perception isn't a delivery system for story—it *is* the story. Every sentence reveals not the world as it is, but the world as someone experiences it.

8.1 The Psychic Distance Dial

The concept of psychic distance, first articulated by John Gardner, refers to the degree of intimacy between narrator and character—the gap between external observation and internal consciousness. You can think of it as a dial that controls how close the reader stands to the mind inside the story. At one end, we hover like a journalist, cool and impartial; at the other, we dissolve into thought itself, feeling every nerve. The skill lies not in choosing one position and holding it rigidly, but in modulating distance to create emotional texture. Just as a film alternates wide shots with close-ups, fiction breathes by expanding and contracting its lens.

Imagine five notches on the dial. At the farthest, the narrator observes from the outside world, describing actions as facts. "It was winter in the city. Commuters hurried through snow." No interiority, only external cues. As the dial turns closer, a second notch allows filtered perception: "He watched the commuters hurry through the snow, their shoulders hunched against the cold." Now we glimpse through a specific consciousness. At the third notch, emotion begins to color observation: "The snow felt endless, as though the city were trying to bury them all." The fourth notch plunges deeper into personal language: "He couldn't feel his fingers anymore, and for a moment he thought maybe that was mercy." At the deepest notch, thought merges with narration entirely: "Can't feel them. Good. Don't have to." The reader now occupies the mind's interior, unmediated.

Each notch changes not only proximity but tone, rhythm, and diction. Far distance invites summary, history, commentary. Close distance favors immediacy, sensory input, the fractured syntax of thought. Mastery of psychic distance means knowing where your story needs heat and where it needs air. Too close for too long, and readers suffocate inside emotion without perspective. Too distant, and the narrative cools into report. The art is in modulation—choosing when to lean in and when to step back.

The most effective shifts occur at moments of **emotional inflection**—shocks, revelations, or spikes of intimacy. During action or crisis, closeness heightens impact. The reader feels the body respond before comprehension catches up. After the moment passes, pulling back allows reflection, context, even irony. This oscillation mimics the human experience of living through events and then interpreting them later. A novel that maintains a single distance throughout feels artificial because consciousness itself doesn't work that way. We inhabit the world in expanding and contracting awareness, sometimes acutely sensory, sometimes abstract and detached. The narrative should echo that rhythm.

Sensory specificity is your lever for closing the distance. When you describe how things *feel, smell, sound,* or *taste,* you anchor the reader inside the body of the point-of-view character. A description like "the room was small" belongs to a distant narrator. Replace it with "his knees brushed the table each time he breathed," and we've entered the body. Texture and temperature are the quickest way to tighten psychic space. Readers translate sensation instantly into empathy.

Abstraction, conversely, pulls the lens back. Generalizations, thematic commentary, and summarizing verbs like "seemed," "felt," or "realized" introduce distance. They belong to the storytelling consciousness rather than the experiencing one. Used sparingly, abstraction offers relief. It allows meaning to surface from raw event. A scene of grief rendered entirely through sobbing and heartbeat risks melodrama; a line of abstract commentary—"Loss reduced everyone to the same grammar"— can reintroduce thought, giving emotion shape. The key is balance. Move between body and mind the way waves move between crest and trough: one rises, the other recedes.

One of the clearest ways to visualize psychic distance is to imagine a camera tracking a subject. At the widest angle, we see the landscape, context, and scale. As we zoom in, detail replaces panorama: faces, hands, breath. Finally, the camera crosses into the subject's interior—the trembling of thought, the flicker of doubt. In fiction, this zoom is achieved not through lens but language. The words you choose determine the aperture. Nouns and verbs denote nearness; adjectives and adverbs tend to belong to the distant observer. "He ran" is inside; "He ran quickly" suggests someone watching from afar.

Manipulating distance also changes authority. A distant narrator carries gravitas, able to comment on the human condition; a close one carries authenticity, able to make the reader *feel* rather than understand. Many great works shift between these modes, letting wisdom and immediacy alternate. In *Middlemarch*, George Eliot's omniscient voice moves seamlessly from philosophical overview to intimate portraiture, giving the novel both moral breadth and psychological depth. In contrast, modern minimalism often keeps the dial near zero, trapping us inside the protagonist's limited awareness to generate realism. Neither extreme is superior; they serve different purposes. The true sophistication lies in the dynamic interplay—moving from close to far so subtly that the reader experiences it as emotion, not technique.

A simple test for distance is to read a passage aloud and note whether it feels like *seeing* or *being*. If you can describe the event as if you were watching it from across the room, you're in the outer notches. If you can't separate observation from reaction—if the language seems to arise from the bloodstream—you've gone deep. Most scenes benefit from beginning at moderate distance to establish clarity, then tightening as stakes rise. The shift itself generates tension, like zooming toward impact.

In revision, mark where each scene sits on the dial. Ask whether the emotional contour matches the level of access. A confession scene written from far away drains intimacy; an action scene rendered in deep interiority may blur spatial logic. Adjust accordingly. Sometimes even one sentence of interior thought can anchor an otherwise detached scene; sometimes one neutral line of description can provide air after suffocating closeness.

Another dimension of psychic distance involves *who* owns the narrative lens. Even within close third person, the narrator and character can diverge slightly. Subtle shifts between their voices create irony and complexity. For instance, a character might think, "He was doing fine," while the narration quietly contradicts through sensory cues: "His hands wouldn't stop shaking." The reader occupies both perspectives at once—the self-deception and the truth. Such duality gives depth without breaking point of view.

Writers often fear inconsistency, but fluid distance is not inconsistency; it's realism. Consciousness itself is inconsistent. We slip between detachment and immersion dozens of times a day. Fiction that mimics that movement feels alive. The key is intentionality—knowing *why* you're shifting. Are you offering relief, revealing irony, or magnifying emotion? The answer determines how far and how fast you move the dial.

Voice, meanwhile, fuses with distance. The closer you go, the more syntax must reflect personality. Word choice becomes fingerprint. Distant narration can afford neutral diction because it speaks from authority; close narration must sound like thought, with all its irregularities, digressions, and contradictions. This is where attitude lives. When voice and psychic distance align, access feels seamless. When they clash—formal narration inside intimate thought—the reader feels the dissonance immediately.

The psychic distance dial is not merely a tool for managing perspective; it's a way of orchestrating emotion. Distance modulates empathy. It allows the writer to pace feeling—drawing the reader in until identification peaks, then releasing them into reflection. It's emotional editing: the heart's zoom lens. And like all good editing, its power lies in rhythm. You don't notice the cuts; you feel the continuity.

At its most refined, control of distance becomes invisible artistry. The reader doesn't think, *Now we're close, now we're far.* They simply experience fluid immersion—an intimacy that feels natural because it mirrors their own interior life. You, the writer, are the unseen hand adjusting the dial, deciding when to whisper and when to step back, when to let language burn with consciousness and when to cool into observation. The result is storytelling that breathes, that thinks, that feels—a narrative capable of both pulse and perspective, alive in the oscillation between seeing and being.

8.2 Unreliability & Trust Management

Every narrator, no matter how sincere, lies a little. The very act of telling a story distorts it. What they notice, what they omit, how they phrase what they remember—all these choices reveal bias. Unreliability isn't only a stylistic device; it's an acknowledgment of human limitation. Readers instinctively know that perception is partial. The writer's task is not to eliminate that fact but to harness it—to turn selective truth into narrative electricity. Trust, in fiction, isn't about accuracy; it's about *consistency of illusion*. The reader must feel that the unreliability belongs to the character's psychology, not the author's negligence.

The foundation of credible unreliability is early calibration. You must signal, even subtly, what kind of distortions the reader can expect. A character who warns us of faulty memory, a first page laced with evasions, a small contradiction between description and dialogue—all act as disclosure clauses in an emotional contract. Once the terms are clear, readers will lean into the gaps, not away from them. They begin reading between the lines, attuned to what the narrator doesn't or can't see. This turns them from passive receivers into active detectives.

Memory gaps are among the most potent sources of controlled unreliability. Forgetting, suppressing, or misremembering can structure a narrative the way negative space structures a painting. The missing pieces invite projection and suspense. Yet you must ground these gaps in psychology, not convenience. Trauma, guilt, obsession, or ideology must make the forgetfulness plausible. When a narrator remembers selectively, we believe it because we recognize the mechanism. Everyone rewrites the past to survive it.

Self-interest provides another engine for distortion. A narrator defending their actions will frame events to justify themselves.

They may exaggerate slights, minimize cruelty, or inflate courage. The reader senses the rhetoric beneath the confession—the performance of virtue—and feels the tension between what's said and what's implied. This tension is the lifeblood of unreliable narration. It creates a second voice beneath the first: the voice of truth trying to break through. The trick is to let the reader discover that secondary voice independently. If the author editorializes or exposes the lie too directly, the spell breaks.

Ideological unreliability operates on a grander scale. A character so steeped in belief—religious, political, cultural—that they interpret every fact through its lens can be terrifyingly persuasive. The reader's horror often stems from recognizing the logic's internal coherence. Such narrators force readers to inhabit a worldview they would otherwise reject, expanding empathy even through discomfort. The danger here is caricature. If ideology turns into sermon or parody, the illusion collapses. Keep the character's convictions emotionally legible; their faith or fanaticism should feel like oxygen to them, not costume to the plot.

To make unreliability compelling rather than confusing, provide **external checks**—secondary evidence, contradictory testimony, or documents that quietly challenge the main account. These can appear as letters, other points of view, marginal notes, or even physical inconsistencies in setting. The goal isn't to disprove the narrator but to create triangulation. Readers enjoy the friction between accounts because it mirrors how truth operates in life: no single witness sees the whole. By layering perspectives, you let readers construct a truth larger than any individual voice.

Think of it as managing tension between *told* and *shown*. The narrator's version of events might sound authoritative, but the physical world betrays them. A man insists his marriage is "as steady as ever," yet he can't remember where his wife keeps the sugar. A teenager swears she feels nothing about her father's death, but she can't stop rearranging his tools. The contradiction between claim and behavior reveals more than any direct confession. This gap—between saying and doing—is the most elegant form of irony. It allows readers to feel smarter than the text without ever feeling manipulated.

You can amplify unreliability by exploiting tone. The more confident a narrator's voice, the more readers scrutinize its cracks. Polished arrogance, over-earnest morality, or excessive certainty all signal self-deception. Conversely, a narrator who admits confusion or guilt often feels more trustworthy, even when they're wrong. Trust and humility are cousins in reader psychology. If your narrator lacks one, give them the other in disguise: a charm, a wit, a vulnerability that keeps empathy alive. Unreliable narrators fail only when readers stop caring whether they're lying. Emotional investment, not accuracy, sustains belief.

The great paradox is that unreliability can make fiction *truer*. By dramatizing how people misperceive and justify, it captures human consciousness more accurately than omniscient precision ever could. We all narrate ourselves into coherence; fiction simply externalizes that universal delusion. What matters is control—knowing the shape of the lie and where its edges blur into truth. A well-managed unreliable narrator is a mirror: we recognize the distortion as our own.

8.3 Multi POV Choreography

If unreliable narration explores the limits of one perspective, multi-point-of-view storytelling explores the orchestra. Each voice becomes an instrument with its own timbre, range, and rhythm. The challenge is not multiplication but differentiation— ensuring that every perspective adds new light rather than echoing the same melody. A well-constructed ensemble of narrators transforms narrative from monologue to symphony, expanding both empathy and tension.

The first step in choreographing multiple points of view is to give each character a *distinct agenda*. A perspective without purpose is filler. Ask what each voice wants the reader to feel, discover, or misunderstand. One narrator might pursue truth, another comfort, another power. Their goals shape their tone, diction, and focus. Readers shouldn't need chapter headers to identify who's speaking; the language itself should announce it. A professor's inner monologue will coil through logic and metaphor, while a child's may leap through sensation and rhythm. Distinction doesn't mean caricature—it means alignment between psychology and syntax.

Vocabulary becomes identity. The words a character selects reveal not only education or background but worldview. Someone who describes a sunset as "a chemical haze" experiences beauty differently than someone who calls it "God's afterthought." Word choice compresses biography. Sentence rhythm, too, becomes fingerprint: clipped for the cautious, sprawling for the impulsive. During revision, test whether you can identify each voice from a paragraph stripped of context. If not, the choreography needs clearer differentiation.

When alternating points of view, think of **purpose tagging** each scene. Every shift should accomplish something specific: discovery, misdirection, or empathy-building. Discovery means revealing new information the previous narrator couldn't access—perhaps an unseen motive or secret event. Misdirection means reinterpreting the same moment from a different emotional truth, showing how perspective alters reality. Empathy-building means deepening connection to a marginalized or misunderstood character. If a POV switch does none of these, it's likely redundancy disguised as complexity.

Transitions between narrators are the connective tissue that keep multi-POV stories coherent. Abrupt jumps disorient unless cushioned by an emotional or imagistic handoff. A shared object—a photograph, a wound, a scent—can bridge consciousness. The chapter might end with one character dropping a letter and the next opening it. A repeated line, question, or sound can serve the same function. Even a shift in weather or setting can thread continuity through contrast. Readers follow emotional resonance more than logic; give them a tether, and they'll cross any structural bridge you build.

Handoff moments also provide opportunities for subtextual communication between narrators. One voice may end on denial, and the next begin by confirming what they refused to see. This creates dialogue across chapters, an invisible conversation that strengthens theme. In ensemble novels like *Atonement* or *Cloud Atlas*, these exchanges create the sense of consciousnesses orbiting a shared moral center. The reader becomes the only participant aware of the full constellation.

To prevent imbalance, track screen time. Too much exposure to one viewpoint can distort the emotional geometry. Each perspective must rise and recede according to the story's heartbeat. Imagine a symphony: sometimes the violins dominate, sometimes percussion, but silence for any instrument too long weakens harmony. Keep a ledger noting which narrator last appeared and why. If two voices serve similar narrative functions—both expository, both reactive—consider merging them or assigning distinct emotional colors. Multiplicity for its own sake dilutes potency.

Multi-POV stories also allow for structural games. You can arrange perspectives linearly, in rotation, or in nested framing. You can withhold one crucial voice until late in the book to reframe everything that came before. Such architecture must serve emotional logic, not gimmick. The reader should feel that each viewpoint expands understanding, not resets it. Too many reversals exhaust trust; too few stagnate curiosity. Balance expansion with synthesis.

A deeper challenge lies in tonal harmony. Distinct voices must still belong to the same world. If one narrator speaks in lyrical introspection while another reports in hard-boiled detachment, find the subtle frequencies that let them coexist—shared imagery, recurring motifs, or mirrored phrasing. These echoes unify without homogenizing. They remind readers that, however divergent the voices, all are bound by the same gravity of theme.

The emotional choreography of multi-POV writing lies in empathy triangulation. The reader aligns with one character, then another, until alliances blur. This moral crossfire generates complexity. In single-viewpoint fiction, empathy is linear; in multi-viewpoint fiction, it's refracted. By forcing the reader to understand incompatible truths simultaneously, you approximate the moral texture of real life. No single voice holds the full picture, but together they form a mosaic of partial certainties.

Managing multiple perspectives also tests discipline in pacing. Each switch resets momentum, so the transitions must justify themselves through escalation or revelation. The reader should sense that the camera shifts because tension demands a new angle. Too frequent changes fracture attention; too infrequent ones risk monotony. The solution lies in rhythm—long arcs punctuated by brief glimpses, crescendos balanced by quiet turns. Think of it as editing film: every cut must preserve continuity of motion, even when moving between entirely different scenes.

Ultimately, multi-POV writing is an act of empathy at scale. It insists that truth is plural and that identity is relational. Each voice exposes a limitation of the others, turning perspective into argument. The writer becomes conductor, not dictator, guiding readers through the dissonance toward harmony. When done well, this orchestration produces a sense of totality—an emotional panorama too vast for any single mind. The story becomes not a line but a field, alive with intersecting voices that argue, echo, and harmonize.

The reader finishes such a book feeling they've inhabited multiple hearts at once, their own perspective subtly rearranged. And that is the ultimate purpose of multi-POV choreography: not to flaunt complexity, but to teach perception—to remind us that every life, every story, is a partial translation of the same human language, spoken with different accents, but yearning toward understanding.

Chapter 9 — Scene Mechanics: Micro Tension That Never Lets Go

Every scene must turn on a small but undeniable change. It doesn't need to be explosive or melodramatic, but it must alter something—an emotion, a relationship, a plan, a belief. Without that micro-turn, a scene is a still life instead of a living moment. Scenes are the heartbeat of narrative, and tension is the electricity that keeps the pulse irregular enough to be interesting. When writers complain that their work "feels flat," they are usually describing scenes that start balanced and end balanced, that drift through conversation or description without disturbance. The reader closes a chapter not because the prose fails, but because nothing shifts. To write scenes that never let go, you must learn to unbalance them deliberately—to walk into the room when energy is already in motion and leave before the dust has settled.

9.1 Off Balance Entries

The first secret of an alive scene is **starting late**. Most drafts begin too early—characters preparing, traveling, greeting, or warming up to the point of conflict. In real life, we often clear our throats before saying what matters; on the page, those gestures steal momentum. Enter after the expected beginning, when something has already started to tilt. Imagine a dinner scene that begins with guests already mid-argument rather than passing the salad. Or a courtroom moment that opens with the witness hesitating under the oath rather than the lawyer calling the case. When you arrive late, you force the reader to lean forward, piecing together context through action instead of explanation. Curiosity replaces orientation.

The mind loves puzzles more than introductions. Dropping readers into a moment of imbalance invites them to decode what preceded it. They become participants rather than spectators. This is why film editors cut directly to the motion of a door already opening instead of showing the hand reaching for the knob. Narrative functions the same way: it's not the act of entering the room that matters, it's the air inside when you arrive. You can always imply the preamble through the first few lines of dialogue or sensory cues. A slammed cupboard tells us a conversation went wrong without summarizing it.

To maintain off-balance momentum, add a **ticking element**, something that quietly counts down inside the scene. The clock doesn't have to be literal; it can be an emotional or environmental constraint. Maybe a storm is closing in, the bus is about to leave, the boss will return in ten minutes, or the truth must be confessed before the plane lands. The countdown may not even be timed— it can be a dwindling resource like trust, oxygen, or patience. What matters is that both the reader and the characters sense that time or stability is eroding. The tick is what keeps dialogue sharp and movement purposeful. Even a calm exchange between lovers gains urgency if one of them has already decided to leave at dawn.

Deadlines generate energy because they limit indecision. Without a countdown, characters can wander through pages of talk; with one, every beat has consequence. The reader's pulse syncs with the implicit clock. This invisible tension works best when the reader senses it but the characters are not all equally aware. Perhaps one person knows time is running out while the other drifts unaware, creating asymmetry and dramatic irony. The ticking element doesn't just hurry the scene; it shapes subtext, revealing who feels the approaching edge and who doesn't.

Another form of tension comes from letting the **setting act as antagonist**. Too many scenes treat place as wallpaper—a static backdrop that neither helps nor hinders. In reality, environments exert pressure. A cramped elevator changes how people argue. A formal dinner constrains what can be said and how loudly. Heat, cold, noise, surveillance, or public scrutiny—all tilt the balance. When space fights back, characters adapt tactics. The scene becomes dynamic because the environment demands strategy.

For example, an argument that would sprawl comfortably in a living room becomes combustible when it happens on a subway platform, surrounded by strangers. A confession that feels intimate in a quiet room turns perilous in an echoing hallway where anyone might overhear. Weather can work the same way. Rain isolates characters under shared shelter; wind scatters their words; heat shortens tempers. Setting isn't neutral; it's an additional player whose temperament you control.

Sometimes the setting itself carries symbolic weight, reinforcing the story's emotional geometry. A conversation about control inside a moving car, a confession in a confessional booth, a power struggle inside a hospital room—the place amplifies the theme. When you design a scene, ask not just *who* is in it, but *where* and *under what rules*. Every space has social gravity. A classroom, a courtroom, a monastery, a nightclub—each dictates posture, tone, and possibility. Breaking those spatial rules becomes rebellion; obeying them becomes constraint. Either way, tension increases because behavior meets boundary.

An off-balance entry also benefits from sensory immediacy. Open with the sound, the texture, the fragment that proves we've walked into the moment mid-breath. "The glass was already broken." "He'd been laughing too hard for anyone to believe it." "The child's question still hung in the air." These are signals that something is already unfolding. They create the impression of life before the page began, a continuum into which we've been granted access. Readers trust a story more when it feels as though it was happening before they arrived.

Equally important is how you control the *angle* of entry. A scene that begins from the emotional inside rather than the logistical outside captures attention faster. Instead of "They gathered in the meeting room at noon," try "By the time everyone sat down, no one wanted to be there." The second version starts at temperature, not coordinates. It tells us about mood, not merely place, and mood is the real arena of tension. An off-balance entry doesn't just jump ahead in time; it jumps to friction.

This approach also helps trim exposition naturally. When you start mid-motion, context filters in through dialogue and observation. Readers don't need a preamble explaining why the characters are there; they need to sense it through what's said, unsaid, or avoided. The scene itself becomes the explanation. Writing this way turns exposition into inference, which is the lifeblood of engagement. A reader who is decoding feels alive inside the text.

However, entering late only works if you plan your **exit** with equal ruthlessness. Because you've stolen the warm-up, you must also deny the cool-down. Leave before resolution lands. The last line of a scene should tilt forward, not sit back. Someone walks away mid-conversation, a question remains unanswered, an emotion goes unspoken. The unbalanced beginning finds its echo in the unbalanced end, keeping the story's current alive. Readers move on not because they're satisfied, but because they need equilibrium restored—and the only way to get it is to read the next page.

Off-balance construction doesn't mean chaos; it means controlled incompleteness. You're designing scenes that feel as though they exist within larger currents, that life extends before and after the slice we see. Each scene should be a cross-section of momentum, not a standalone tableau. The craft lies in how much you withhold and how sharply you focus on the collision point. Think of it like photography: the edges are blurred, but the center glows with contrast.

To achieve this, imagine your scene as a tug-of-war that's already mid-pull. One side is winning by inches, the rope is taut, and we can see the strain on every knuckle. You don't need to show how they took their positions; you need to show the moment when the balance begins to shift. That's where micro tension lives—in the second before something gives way. It might be a word, a gesture, or a look that changes who holds power. But something must tip.

At its core, the principle of off-balance entry respects the reader's intelligence. It assumes they can catch up and even enjoy catching up. It honors pacing by trusting inference over explanation. It also mirrors how experience actually feels: we step into ongoing situations, we rarely get full context, we read rooms in motion. When scenes imitate that real-time urgency, they acquire authenticity. The page breathes at the same tempo as life.

To build a story out of such scenes means each one carries an ember of friction. You light it by starting late, you feed it with a ticking element, and you fan it with environment. No single spark must become an inferno, but the combined glow keeps readers warm enough to stay. That's what micro tension is—not explosion, but sustained charge. Every time you deny balance, you create the desire for restoration. That desire is narrative hunger. It doesn't let go because the reader doesn't want it to. And as long as you feed that small, undeniable change—the constant flicker of instability—your scenes will never drift, and your story will never fall asleep.

9.2 Beat Taxonomy & Status Moves

Every scene is a duel disguised as a conversation. Beneath the surface of dialogue and description, characters are constantly negotiating—trying to gain ground, protect themselves, or redirect the flow of power. This invisible calculus of advantage, loss, and recovery is what keeps scenes alive even when nothing "happens." To write with sustained micro tension, you must think not in sentences but in **beats**—small tactical units of interaction. Each beat shifts energy between participants. Every line, every glance, every silence is a move on the board.

A beat functions like a pulse: it marks change. The moment one character makes an **offer**—a piece of information, an invitation, an emotion—the other must respond. That response could be a **demand**, a **challenge**, a **concession**, or a **pivot**. The interplay of these beats forms the rhythm of the scene. When both characters' goals align, energy drains; when they cross, energy spikes. Skilled writers never allow equilibrium to last more than a few lines. Someone must always be slightly off balance, recalibrating.

Imagine a conversation between two old friends. One wants forgiveness, the other wants justification. The first line is an offer: "I should have called." The second is a challenge: "You think that would've fixed anything?" Already, the power dynamic shifts. A third beat—a pivot—could redirect the tone: "Maybe not. But I wanted you to hear it from me." Each new move redefines what's at stake. The reader feels tension not from external conflict but from these micro reversals of control.

Tracking **status**—who is "up" or "down" at any given moment—turns this abstract rhythm into measurable motion. Every interaction in fiction carries a status transaction, even when unspoken. A compliment can be an elevation; a question can be a test; silence can be dominance disguised as restraint. The person who controls rhythm controls status. When one character dictates pace—cutting another off, changing subject, withholding answers—they're asserting control. When they stumble, hesitate, or overexplain, status drops.

You can test a scene's tension by examining its final beat. Ask yourself: who walks away with greater control? Who has been disarmed? If status at the end matches status at the start, the scene hasn't turned. Even quiet scenes need this motion. A teacher consoling a student may begin as authority and end as confessor. A detective interviewing a suspect may leave less certain than when he began. The shift need not be large; it just needs to register as imbalance.

Interruptions and refusals are the bloodstream of beat dynamics. A clean, uninterrupted conversation is almost always dead on the page because it fulfills expectations. When one character interrupts another, the reader's nervous system spikes. The rhythm breaks, and so does composure. Similarly, when a character refuses to answer, change subject, or engage, tension compounds. Silence, when placed between an offer and a demand, functions as both shield and weapon. Readers instinctively lean forward to fill the gap, projecting anxiety into it.

The paradox of scene construction is that resolution kills momentum. Every time characters reach full understanding, tension dissipates. To maintain propulsion, let each exchange close on partial answers. Leave emotional residue unresolved. The next scene can pick up that energy and redirect it. Great serial storytellers understand this implicitly: each conversation ends not with agreement but with a new question or suspicion. Resolution belongs to the final chapter, not the middle ones.

This approach requires precision in dialogue pacing. The first draft of any scene often feels flat because all beats share the same emotional temperature. Revision means modulating heat: vary volume, tone, and reaction time. A sudden concession after prolonged resistance surprises. A delayed response after apparent surrender recharges curiosity. Think of your beats as musical notes; silence, repetition, and variation create rhythm.

Equally vital is attention to *tactical* motivation. Every beat, even a single word, should pursue a micro-objective: to persuade, deflect, assert, or conceal. When characters lose tactical purpose, their lines become filler. To diagnose weak beats, remove them and check whether the emotional trajectory changes. If it doesn't, the line was static noise. Tighten until every move changes the power equation.

Physicality reinforces status moves. Body language contradicts or amplifies dialogue, revealing unspoken reversals. A character rising from a chair midway through an argument seizes vertical dominance. A smile delivered after insult can humiliate more than anger. Use gestures sparingly but strategically—each one should echo a shift in control. When body and voice align perfectly, tension peaks; when they diverge, subtext deepens.

By treating each exchange as tactical combat, you ensure that even domestic scenes hum with energy. A couple discussing groceries can carry the same voltage as a duel if each line subtly maneuvers for reassurance, attention, or reprisal. What matters is not the topic but the shifting current beneath it. That current—status rising and falling—creates narrative electricity that arcs from paragraph to paragraph.

9.3 Dialogue as Action (Subtext)

Dialogue is not conversation. It is action disguised as speech—characters pushing, hiding, testing, seducing, defending. Every line should *do* something, not merely *say* something. The writer's goal is to make readers feel that words are weapons and shields, that talk is a battlefield where control and vulnerability trade places. What gives dialogue its charge is **subtext**—the gap between what's said and what's meant. Subtext is the current that hums beneath polite language, transforming civility into combat.

To craft dialogue that acts, you must first strip it bare. Write an initial draft where characters speak bluntly, stating motives directly. Then perform a "said less" pass: remove every explicit admission and replace it with implication. People rarely announce their desires; they orbit them. A line like "I still love you" might become "You didn't even ask if I was seeing anyone." The surface text shifts from confession to accusation, but the emotional truth remains. Subtext emerges through displacement—emotion redirected into another register.

Once intention replaces information, clarity must return through texture: gestures, rhythm, or setting details that reveal undercurrent. A character polishing glasses while insisting "I'm fine" makes denial visible. A pause before a simple "Sure" carries more weight than a paragraph of confession. The fewer words you use, the more readers supply their own meaning. That participation creates engagement; the reader becomes co-author of emotional truth.

Objects are powerful conduits for subtext. A cup, a coat, a key— each can carry unspoken emotion when handled with intention. A woman passing a mug across a table can communicate apology, avoidance, or tenderness depending on the preceding tension. These small physical anchors translate abstract emotion into tactile action. When language lies, objects tell the truth. They bridge the psychological gap between dialogue and inner life, grounding tension in sensory reality.

Silence, too, is dialogue. A withheld response is not emptiness; it's pressure concentrated. The pause after a question can convey hesitation, contempt, or grief. Measured correctly, silence forces the other character—and the reader—to fill the void. It transforms reading from observation to participation. The greatest dramatists understood this instinctively: what isn't said carries the heaviest weight.

Redirected answers are another key to living dialogue. People rarely respond directly to what's asked; they reframe or deflect to protect themselves. This misalignment keeps scenes unpredictable. When every question receives its logical answer, tension flatlines. Let your characters talk past each other. Allow misunderstanding to become rhythm. The reader will lean forward, trying to reconcile competing truths. This interpretive engagement is the heartbeat of subtext.

Narration must complement, not duplicate, dialogue. When a line of speech reveals emotion, the narration that follows should offer contrast or consequence, not explanation. If a character says, "I'm not angry," the narration shouldn't confirm it; it should reveal the tremor in their hand or the calculated calm in their tone. Contrast deepens complexity. Redundancy flattens it. The interplay between what's said and what's observed creates three-dimensional emotion.

Dialogue as action also depends on timing. The rhythm of response—the lag between line and line—communicates more than the content itself. Quick exchanges suggest control battles or chemistry; slow ones suggest introspection, discomfort, or deceit. Even punctuation manipulates this rhythm. A dash can interrupt; ellipses can trail anxiety; a period after a curt phrase can land like a slap. The writer who hears dialogue as music controls its psychological tempo.

Subtext thrives in collisions between inner motive and outer mask. Each character's speech should reveal the effort of self-concealment. Desire leaks through denials, anger through politeness, fear through humor. Instead of writing "She was nervous," let her talk too much. Instead of "He wanted to leave," let him check his watch, then smile as if enjoying himself. Readers recognize these contradictions instantly—they mimic real life. We live inside the dissonance between what we express and what we feel.

Revision is where subtext solidifies. After drafting dialogue, reread it aloud. If every line communicates exactly what it appears to, it's exposition, not tension. Look for opportunities to bury motive one layer deeper. Replace certainty with ambiguity. Let characters interrupt themselves, trail off, or shift tone mid-sentence. These imperfections humanize speech and make emotion kinetic. A perfect sentence rarely feels alive; a flawed one, spoken under pressure, does.

Ultimately, dialogue achieves power not by cleverness but by necessity. When words become the only available weapon or refuge, they pulse with urgency. In such moments, every phrase carries consequence—what is spoken cannot be unsaid. That's when readers lean in, sensing danger in language itself. The most gripping scenes aren't the loudest but the ones where talk teeters on revelation, where each syllable might change a relationship's future. Dialogue, at its best, is a form of action so intimate it leaves bruises we can't see.

Chapter 10 — Revision Pipeline: From Rough to Relentless

Drafts discover; revisions decide. The first draft is an act of exploration, a conversation between instinct and possibility. The revision process, by contrast, is architecture—an exacting sequence of decisions that transforms raw material into precision. It is where the novel becomes intentional, where accidents are either exploited or erased. Too many writers approach revision as cleanup—grammar, polish, surface correction. But true revision means re-visioning: seeing the work anew through multiple lenses. Each pass answers a different question. What is this book promising? Where does it falter? Which moments of emotion deserve magnification, and which must vanish for rhythm's sake? The **diagnostic pass** is where this triage begins—the part of the pipeline that turns chaos into craft.

10.1 Diagnostic Passes

The first read after a completed draft should never be surgical; it should be diagnostic. Imagine you are a doctor meeting a patient who's just survived a long ordeal—you don't rush to operate; you assess symptoms, vital signs, and systems. The goal of a diagnostic pass is to map strengths and weaknesses before touching a word. If drafting was improvisation, diagnosis is listening. The book will tell you where it hurts if you're patient enough to let it speak.

Start with the **global scan**. Read the manuscript from beginning to end, ideally on a different medium than you wrote it. Print it, or read it on an e-reader, anything that shifts your brain from composition mode to evaluation mode. As you read, resist the urge to line-edit. You're not adjusting sentences—you're interrogating architecture. Ask: does the story deliver the promise made on page one? Every narrative makes a tacit agreement with the reader through tone and setup. A novel that opens with a corpse on the sidewalk pledges discovery or justice. A novel that opens with a breakup promises emotional transformation. If the middle or ending drift from that initial contract, the story feels faithless, even if individual scenes glitter. The global pass is about honoring that invisible handshake.

Next, confirm **genre signals**. Each genre carries a pattern of reader expectation—mystery demands revelation, romance demands intimacy and renewal, speculative fiction demands consequence. You can subvert these conventions only after acknowledging them. Mark where your manuscript announces genre too faintly or too loudly. A thriller whose tension deflates at midpoint needs more escalation; a character drama masquerading as crime fiction must decide which identity to commit to. The global pass is your opportunity to align promise with delivery, tone with outcome.

While reading, pay attention to the **value shift** at the heart of the story. Every complete narrative moves from one state to another: ignorance to knowledge, fear to courage, isolation to belonging. Without that pivot, a novel feels static no matter how eventful it is. Identify the emotional polarity of your tale and note where it turns. You should be able to articulate this shift in one sentence: "The protagonist moves from secrecy to confession," or "The world changes from illusion to clarity." This is not marketing copy—it's the compass that keeps every subsequent revision oriented.

Now examine the **middle stretch**, the notorious graveyard of momentum. Most manuscripts sag after the initial spark because goals blur, stakes plateau, or subplots multiply without consequence. During the diagnostic phase, flag every chapter that could be removed without altering the ending. If more than one fits, your middle is soft. Don't cut yet—just mark the redundancy. Later passes will determine whether these sections can be compressed or repurposed to reveal something new. A strong middle should feel like tightening gravity, not an intermission.

Once the global pulse is measured, move to the **structural pass**. This is where you dissect chronology, scene order, and transitions. Spread the manuscript across a surface—literal or digital—and outline what actually happens, not what you think happens. Writers often discover that emotional beats repeat or major revelations arrive too late to influence outcome. Reordering scenes can rescue pacing more efficiently than rewriting. Look for delayed entries and premature exits. Many chapters begin three paragraphs too early, warming up toward the true conflict. Likewise, many scenes linger after the emotional turn, repeating what the reader already knows. Trimming these excess edges gives the narrative velocity without sacrificing depth.

During this stage, consider merging **duplicative scenes**—moments that perform identical functions. Two arguments that reveal the same rift, two chases that prove the same threat, two memories that explain the same wound. Keep the stronger one and harvest details from the weaker. Repetition dulls emotional impact. A single clean wound hurts more than a dozen shallow cuts. Streamlining structure is not about brevity; it's about clarity of force.

Structural revision also tests continuity of escalation. Each major scene should build on the previous one's consequence. If your protagonist faces equivalent challenges in sequence—three similar fights, three similar heartbreaks—the curve flattens. Raise not only external stakes but emotional ones. What costs increase with each decision? A diagnostic outline helps you visualize these arcs in miniature. Seeing your story as a sequence of consequences transforms it from collection to chain reaction.

After structure comes the **continuity audit**, the least glamorous but most essential step. Continuity anchors credibility. Readers will forgive leaps of faith in premise but not in logic. Cross-check your timeline—days of the week, travel durations, weather patterns. Confirm that minor props remain consistent: a blue car doesn't become red, a broken phone doesn't reappear functional. Maintain a living **change log** as you revise, especially if you adjust chronology or merge scenes. One alteration in chapter four can ripple through twenty others. The log protects you from invisible contradictions.

Continuity extends to emotional realism as well. A character who endures trauma cannot revert to normal behavior two pages later without consequence. Track emotional states as meticulously as physical ones. If someone experiences betrayal, note when and how trust rebuilds—or if it ever does. Readers measure truth by psychological coherence more than factual accuracy. The continuity pass ensures that the inner timeline of healing, fatigue, or obsession aligns with external events.

These diagnostic passes—global, structural, continuity—constitute the skeleton of the revision pipeline. But they also serve a subtler purpose: they distance you from the ego of creation. The first draft belongs to the dreamer; revision belongs to the craftsman. The diagnostic process allows you to treat the manuscript as object rather than mirror, to analyze its mechanics without collapsing into self-judgment. By approaching revision as a series of systems checks, you replace the panic of imperfection with method.

Once diagnosis is complete, only then can you operate. The next phases—line rhythm, image economy, dialogue precision—will refine language, but without this initial assessment they risk polishing flaws that should have been rebuilt. The diagnostic stage doesn't demand solutions; it demands honesty. A good revision map begins not with certainty but with awareness: here the promise wavers, here structure bloats, here emotion rings false. The courage to see the book's fractures without flinching is what separates amateurs who endlessly tinker from professionals who transform.

At the end of this pass, you should have a dossier rather than a rewritten text—a document of observations, flagged pages, and questions. The novel will look wounded, exposed, but clearer than ever before. You'll know where to cut, where to deepen, where to reorder. The next stages of the pipeline will address each in turn, but for now, resist the urge to fix. Diagnosis is not about doing; it's about understanding. Only by knowing the precise nature of the problem can revision become what it was always meant to be: not repair, but deliberate evolution.

10.2 Reader Feedback Systems

Revision often happens in solitude, but the truth is that no writer can fully diagnose their own blind spots. After months or years inside a project, the story's logic becomes invisible—you no longer read what's on the page but what you meant to write. This is where **reader feedback systems** become crucial. They act as external sensors detecting where attention drops, confusion blooms, or emotion ignites. Yet feedback, if unmanaged, can harm more than it helps. Most beta readers default to opinion rather than observation, and a flood of vague advice ("I liked it," "The ending felt off") leaves the writer lost. The solution is to replace unstructured commentary with a **protocol**, a system that turns reactions into usable data.

The beta protocol begins with a single directive: never ask readers whether they *liked* your story. "Like" is irrelevant. What you need to know is *when* they were bored, confused, or thrilled. These three emotional coordinates chart the reader's actual experience—attention (boredom), comprehension (confusion), and investment (thrill). Every other piece of feedback can be translated into one of these. A note like "The dialogue dragged" means boredom; "I didn't get why she left" means confusion; "I couldn't put it down here" signals thrill. By narrowing the vocabulary, you channel chaos into pattern. Readers become sensors, not critics.

During beta rounds, ask readers to mark pages live, either on a digital document or a printout. Encourage gut responses, not essays. "I zoned out here," "Had to reread," "Loved this twist." These raw signals—when aggregated—create a map of engagement more reliable than subjective praise. Once you collect responses, visualize them as a **heatmap**: yellow for boredom, red for confusion, green for thrill. When you step back and see clusters of color, patterns emerge. If three readers turn yellow across the same twenty pages, you've found a dead zone. If green spikes near the climax but fades during transitions, you've diagnosed pacing issues. The heatmap doesn't judge; it reveals where energy lives and dies.

Clusters are triage cues. Fix them before chasing small stylistic complaints. A perfect sentence won't save a dull scene. Look first at yellow—boredom. Boredom usually means stakes have gone static or repetition has dulled surprise. Trim or condense those sections, reframe them around tension rather than exposition. Red—confusion—often arises from missing connective tissue: unclear goals, sudden POV shifts, inconsistent timelines. Insert brief clarifiers rather than long explanations; readers prefer orientation, not lectures. Green—thrill—is the gold vein. Study what generates it: rhythm, revelation, emotional truth. Once identified, replicate its DNA elsewhere in the manuscript.

Sometimes fixing one color cures another. A confused reader quickly becomes a bored one, and an engaged reader forgives minor confusion. The goal isn't to eliminate yellow and red entirely—no story can sustain constant green—but to manage rhythm. Contrast creates momentum. A quiet yellow stretch between two green bursts can serve as rest. What matters is intentionality: you must control the pulse, not surrender to it.

For key scenes, employ **A/B testing**, a technique borrowed from design and marketing but astonishingly effective in writing. Create two versions of a pivotal moment—perhaps the confrontation, the reveal, or the emotional climax. One may use summary, the other dramatization; one might start later, the other earlier. Give each to different beta readers *blind*, without telling them they're alternatives. Ask only: "At what point did you lean forward?" The version that provokes more sustained attention wins. A/B testing converts intuition into evidence. It's not democracy; it's data-guided refinement.

Feedback, however, demands discernment. Even structured reactions can mislead if misinterpreted. Readers can identify symptoms but not always causes. When multiple readers are confused by the same passage, don't assume the information missing is what they suggest adding. Often the fix lies earlier—foreshadowing clarity, sharpening motivation, or adjusting pacing. Treat every note as a clue, not a command. The writer's job is to find the structural reason behind the symptom.

Similarly, remember that readers differ in focus. Some are emotional sensors; others notice logic or language. Assign roles deliberately. One beta might track character consistency, another world-building plausibility, another sentence rhythm. Diversity of reader type creates triangulation, reducing personal bias. And once you integrate changes, conduct a second mini-round—not to re-litigate everything, but to ensure new fixes didn't introduce fresh confusion. Revision is iteration, not overhaul.

Finally, protect your creative core. Feedback is a mirror, not a master. The most dangerous stage of revision comes after praise fades and criticism accumulates. The temptation is to chase every suggestion, sanding off the story's individuality until only consensus remains. Resist. The purpose of feedback systems is to refine *your* intent, not replace it. Keep a document labeled "Keeper's Creed," listing the three truths of your book—the emotional promise, the character journey, the thematic spine. When feedback tempts you to stray, reread those sentences. They're the compass through noise.

10.3 Line Level Craft

Once structure, pacing, and logic are sound, revision zooms into language—the realm of rhythm, precision, and echo. The line-level pass transforms clarity into cadence, converting prose from functional to alive. This stage demands microscopic attention but macro patience. You are tuning the instrument note by note until it sings without calling attention to itself.

The first task is **concreteness**. Abstract adjectives and vague modifiers are symptoms of fatigue. Replace them with nouns and verbs that embody the sensation directly. Instead of "a very sad expression," write "her mouth sagged as if speech were a burden." Instead of "a beautiful sunset," describe "clouds bleeding coral into the bay." Concrete language doesn't just describe; it conjures. Each substitution tightens emotional circuitry between text and reader. Abstract language generalizes; concrete language personalizes.

In close point of view, eliminate **filter verbs**—phrases that remind the reader of the character's observation instead of letting them experience it. Words like *saw, felt, noticed, realized* act as panes of glass between consciousness and sensation. "She felt the wind against her face" distances us; "The wind stung her cheek" dissolves mediation. Revision at this level is often subtraction: remove the unnecessary intermediaries until perception becomes direct experience.

Next comes rhythm. Prose breathes through variation, and rhythm is its respiratory system. Examine sentence openings; too many beginning with the same structure ("He walked," "He looked," "He thought") create monotony. Rearrange syntax, start with subordinate clauses or sensory detail. Variety in rhythm generates forward motion without the reader noticing why. Read aloud. The ear catches dullness the eye forgives. If your tongue trips, the reader's mind will too.

Watch for **duplicate beats**, moments where emotion or description repeats with slight rephrasing. They often arise from drafting momentum—writers restating an idea because they don't yet trust its impact. In revision, compress or merge them. Repetition dulls power. If a paragraph contains two sentences that express the same tension, delete the safer one. Prose becomes relentless not by addition but by absence of hesitation.

At the same time, avoid flattening texture. Rhythmic monotony can result from over-tightening, producing a uniform staccato. Alternate pulse: long sentences expanding emotion, short ones puncturing it. Cadence mirrors consciousness—thought rushes when panicked, drifts when reflective. The best line-level revision aligns syntax with psychology.

Beyond clarity and rhythm lies resonance—the subtle craft of **motif callback**. The final ten percent of a story is where meaning crystallizes. Readers don't need everything repeated, but they crave recognition: an image or phrase reappearing transformed by context. A lamp described as "unlit" in chapter one glowing faintly in the finale; a repeated metaphor shifting implication from loss to acceptance. These callbacks bind emotional circuitry without overt explanation. The key is modulation. Too direct a repetition feels manipulative; too subtle and it goes unnoticed. Aim for the reader's subconscious—the flicker of *I've been here before, but everything's changed.*

Line-level work also involves rhythm between narration and white space. Paragraph breaks control tempo more than punctuation ever could. A dense paragraph traps the reader in thought; a single-line paragraph releases tension. Manipulate space intentionally: cluster sentences for claustrophobia, scatter them for vulnerability. On the page, structure is sound made visible.

Metaphor, too, demands pruning. In early drafts, metaphors often accumulate like weeds—each lovely alone, but choking flow together. Choose the one that carries thematic weight and cut the rest. When imagery recurs across chapters, ensure it evolves; a stagnant metaphor stalls emotional growth. Precision isn't austerity; it's focus.

This stage is also where diction merges with character. Each viewpoint should inflect language slightly differently, even in third person. The rhythm of their thinking should shape the prose: a soldier's clipped syntax, a poet's sensory layering, a scientist's analytical cadence. Revision at the sentence level should refine this alignment until no line could belong to anyone else's story.

As you near the end, read the manuscript aloud once more—not for grammar, but for momentum. Listen for drag. Each paragraph should carry energy into the next, propelled by tension or curiosity. When a line ends flat, adjust rhythm or imagery until it hums. Relentless prose is not breathless; it's alive with momentum, its energy regenerating with every clause.

Finally, guard against perfection paralysis. The closer you get, the more microscopic your scrutiny, the more tempting it becomes to tinker endlessly. At some point, improvement turns to erosion. Recognize the moment when the prose's pulse feels steady—when no sentence jars, when images align like constellations, when reading aloud feels like following current rather than forging it. That's the signal: the work is ready to meet readers. Revision has done its job—not to sterilize the manuscript, but to restore it to the clarity it was always reaching for.

Printed by Libri Plureos GmbH in Hamburg, Germany